# Marriage

# Faithful Lovers in God

***You, Your Marriage, and Your Family in God's side***

**By**

**Philippe Remy**

# Contents

Introduction ........ xviii

You, your marriage, and your family in God's side ........ 1

The spirituality of the Church ........ 1

How to live your marriage in difficult circumstances (times)? ........ 2

Your marriage and the culture ........ 2

Couples living next to strangers ........ 3

According to the Bible, Christians should never be divided among themself (keep the Marriage Holy) ........ 3

The responsibility of the believer in the Marriage ........ 4

God wants his people to live in peace ........ 5

Return to the ancient love (the first Gospel) ........ 5

Your marriage needs to be a model to the Pagans ........ 5

Bibliography ........ 6

Husband, love your wives as Christ loved the Church ........ 6

A marriage ceremony is a victory for the couple in our society today ........ 7

Why it is important to respect your husband ........ 8

Choose your partner according to your faith in God. Your spouse is for life ........ 8

It is not really my viewpoint, but it is according to the Bible ........ 9

Marriage is instituted by God. Genesis 2:18-25 ........ 10

God's design for Christian marriage ........ 10

God's personal relationship with the creation ........ 11

A contrast, (It is not good and it is good) ........ 12

Marriage is instituted by God. Genesis 2:18- 25 ........ 12

God's direction on marriage ........ 13

Marriage in the Garden of Eden ........ 14

Feminism does not let ladies be a helper ........ 14

Preach salvation in your marriage ........ 15

Feminism destroys Marriage in the 21st century ........ 15

Equality in marriage but distinct roles to fulfill .............................. 16
The husband must treat his wife as his own body .............................. 16
In marriage, the wife fulfills the husband's needs in all .............................. 17
A gift from God that the husband needs to appreciate .............................. 18
The first man on the face of the earth, as he sees his wife .............................. 19
He cherished her as a very part of himself and saw his wife as God's exquisite gift to him .............................. 20
God Designed Marriage. Genesis 2:18-25. .............................. 21
Marriage makes the spouse holy in spite of sexuality .............................. 22
Marriage protects Christians against sin .............................. 22
Your choice as Christians (Who will be your Spouse?) .............................. 23
In case you have just converted to the Christian faith .............................. 23
What would you do? .............................. 23
Facts about an unbeliever .............................. 24
God wants everyone to be saved, as it says .............................. 24
Evangelize your Family .............................. 25
Live by example .............................. 25
Money and the Marriage .............................. 26
Testimony of a Queen with her husband .............................. 26
It is important to have fun .............................. 27
Maturity in the choice .............................. 27
Quality of a good husband (character) .............................. 28
Build up the partnership .............................. 28
Man's responsibility is not relying on the wife .............................. 29
A Godly man is a protector .............................. 29
A real man knows the Bible .............................. 30
Good examples for married people .............................. 30
Do you want a secret about marriage? .............................. 31
The things to talk about in marriage .............................. 31
Not about winning but about God's will .............................. 32
How to forgive and forget in marriage .............................. 32

The outcome of marriage ... 33
Details about disagreements ... 33
A husband's behavior in marriage ... 34
Better communication in the marriage ... 34
See yourself in the mirror ... 35
The foundation of marriage ... 36
The Marriage from the Bible ... 36
Commitment is what bound the partners in marriage ... 37
Do not doubt yourself if your marriage is not working ... 37
The effective way of living with your spouse ... 38
It is Good ... 38
Effective communication skills. ... 39
Do not live today in the future. ... 39
Promise in the marriage ... 39
Being honest ... 40
What really changes after one or two, or three days? ... 40
Date the perfect person. ... 40
Open your eyes and meet that person ... 42
Healthy Habit ... 42
Compatibility in choosing your partner ... 42
God can choose for you ... 43
A sign or a Vision ... 43
Love is not a cultural topic but a biblical one ... 44
He that loved his wife loved himself ... 44
It is the man's responsibility to be involved in his wife's affairs ... 46
Man, God has given you control as the head of the home ... 46
Repeat the love habit through the ages ... 47
You must be concerned about your wife and your children's wellbeing ... 47
Violation of the covenant obligations ... 47
Financial obligations ... 48

Marriage in ancient times and marriage today ................................ 48
A plan is necessary ............................................................. 49
Today's Marriage ................................................................ 49
Concern about her well-being ................................................... 50
God expects you to nourish her ................................................ 51
When people have issues, they cannot live healthily ...................... 51
When people have issues, they cannot live healthily ...................... 52
Disagreement in marriage ........................................................ 53
Communication problems ......................................................... 53
How a wife perceives the husband ............................................. 54
Obedience in the relationship ................................................... 55
Who's fault is it? ................................................................... 56
God communicates to us ......................................................... 57
Marriage is for everyone who believes according to the will of God ................................................................................................ 58
Wrong motives in marriage ..................................................... 58
Marriage and Money .............................................................. 59
You are the house born; that is why they call you a father ............. 59
It is natural for the man to call his wife "baby." ............................ 60
The family is like a business corporation .................................. 60
Man must be the boss of the home ............................................ 61
How is the marriage going to be successful? ................................ 61
Each partner is there to make the other happy .............................. 62
Stop blaming the other partner ................................................. 63
Negotiation can save your marriage .......................................... 63
The purpose you are getting married ......................................... 63
Why did you want to get married? ............................................ 64
Love and its barriers .............................................................. 65
The love you give allows God's love to flow at greater levels ........ 65
What is the secret to a healthy and happy marriage? ..................... 66
The answer for a happy marriage .............................................. 66

A healthy marriage is to root out the spirit of competition............. 67
Until you have children............................................................ 68
Think twice, plan your marriage................................................ 68
Doctor Philippe's answer.......................................................... 69
The mood ................................................................................ 69
Complaining husband ................................................................ 70
A little talk about baby or considerations ................................... 71
Dilemma.................................................................................... 72
The most fundamental conception of humankind........................... 74
Some advice about breaking the marriage engagement.................. 74
Those are details not from the Bible ........................................... 75
What takes away the peace? If love is there, peace is not there (Not the Biblical)........................................................................................ 75
Helpful details but not from the Bible .......................................... 76
Helpful details but not from the Bible .......................................... 77
Conciseness............................................................................... 77
What makes a marriage a marriage?............................................ 78
Marriage Commitment................................................................ 79
God makes it clear it is a real covenant ....................................... 80
Protect your soul, get married...................................................... 80
Many of us want perfection in the church ................................... 81
Looking for perfection ................................................................ 82
What does the Bible say about marriage?..................................... 82
Marriage was created by God ...................................................... 83
A biblical principle that was right at the beginning of creation, for example, Genesis 2:24 ............................................................. 83
Christian's experience redeeming quality ...................................... 84
God does not want Christians to marry non-Christians.................. 85
God created marriage to avoid polygamy...................................... 85
The Bible says premarital sex is a sin. What God has joined together, let no man separate ................................................................... 86

The Bible says that marriage is a symbolic representation of the relationship between Christ and the Church .................................... 87

Marriage is between a man and a woman. A man and a woman are married in God's eyes when they have completed some kind of formal wedding .................................................................................... 88

The marriage needs a contract signed by both parties in order to be legally enforceable ...................................................................................... 88

Marriage regulations around the world today ................................. 89

Marriage, according to the Bible, is a man and a woman married in God's eyes .............................................................................................. 89

Every Greek culture in the history of humanity has seen some kind of formal wedding. John chapter 22; Jesus was present at a wedding ceremony ............................................................................................ 90

Every married couple is not truly married in God's eyes ................ 90

The difference between a real wife from a concubine 2 chronicles Chapter 11 verse 20 .......................................................................... 91

Example of a couple being married solely by sexual intercourse without a wedding ceremony ........................................................... 91

Marriage today versus marriage in ancient times ........................... 92

The things we talk about are how to make your marriage better and better every day ................................................................................. 92

Isaac and Rebecca were married with no certificate or paperwork, so how should Christians define marriage today ................................. 93

They made a committed commitment to each other that is recorded in Genesis 20 ................................................................................... 94

Marriage commitment to each other before God (vow) ................. 94

You must go through what is called solemnization ........................ 95

What should I do about my spouse or partner with a nonbeliever... 95

Testimony of an "Unbeliever" converted to Christian Life ............ 96

Nonbeliever's testimony ................................................................... 96

Nonbeliever details ........................................................................... 97

Always believing in God ................................................................. 98

Jesse's salvation story ....................................................................... 98

Jesse came home after I packed his bags and said give me one more chance. (Conversion) .................... 99

Someone might not be a Christian, but that does not mean they cannot have good behavior .................... 100

Christians do not marry nonchristians .................... 101

Have a marriage ministry .................... 101

I had to see him as a brother in Christ, she said .................... 102

God's perspective for our marriage .................... 103

God wants me to be happy .................... 103

God cares about my spouse, and he wants us to be happy. He wants me to walk out of my life a certain way, to be a ministry in my home .................... 104

She did say she set boundaries in that relationship, but she did not stop loving him. She did not stop praying for him and preaching to him .................... 104

The husband stands for Christ, and that is the symbol of that marriage .................... 105

That he reconciled me, that he is given me the Holy Spirit, and so you have the symbol of marriage being a symbol of the gospel, Jesus Christ, and the Church .................... 106

Minister in your home .................... 106

He goes to the people that are unequally yoked .................... 107

A woman has a husband who is an unbeliever, and he can sense to live with her, she should not divorce him .................... 108

Now suddenly, the holy spirits come into the world. Jesus Christ on the cross and people are getting saved .................... 108

To the rest of you who have come to the Lord and your spouse has not. This is how you should live, but he says so. He says if your unbelieving spouse does not want to leave meaning, you are to marry .................... 109

If the unbeliever wants to leave, let him or her do so .................... 109

You are preaching the gospel to them every single day. You are loving them, you are encouraging them, you are praying for them 110

Who knows, husbands, if your unbelieving wife will not get saved because of your life .................... 110

Your example could potentially save your spouse. ....................... 111

Because you are practicing righteousness before your spouse. ..... 112

I should say speak to your spouse 24/7 about what the word says enter and convince them to become a Christian that actions are so powerful. ......................................................................... 112

We treat our spouses the way the Bible tells us to treat them........ 113

The husband recognizes, like Oh my gosh, I am going to walk with my wife in an understanding way. I am going to show her that I understand her. I am going to work to teach her and love her....... 113

We are supposed to look at the world; we do not look at it through just our own opinions or even through just our own experiences.. 114

Believers, you know, so the point is not just to have a comfortable, happy marriage, the point is to be holy, and the point is the salvation of your spouse's soul is the most important thing. ......................... 115

It's true that Jesus came to save us. He reconciles us with the father so we can have a great relationship with him. Without Jesus, we can't save ourselves. ........................................................... 115

You should believe today that you love so much that they would share the gospel that they want you to be saved. .......................... 116

Rejoice in persecution. People who believe in Jesus rejoice because of the hope they have and so, like I said, this gospel is not just that we would have a happy, comfortable life now, but that we have eternal hope in Jesus Christ........................................................ 116

What fellowship does light have with darkness?........................... 117

Working in the same direction. .................................................. 117

Going to church does not mean being a Christian. ....................... 118

To be married less will be called singleness more will be called to marriage, so marriage is right. .................................................. 119

He must not divorce her. ............................................................ 119

How do you know if you, as a wife, will save your husband, or how do you know if you, as a husband, will save your wife? .............. 120

The Bible advises against divorcing an unequally yoked spouse. Once you make a covenant commitment with someone, God wants you to honor that commitment and avoid divorce. ....................... 120

Your example could potentially save your spouse. ....................... 121

Because you are practicing righteousness before your spouse...... 121

I should say speak to your spouse 24/7 about what the word says enter and convince them to become a Christian that actions are so powerful. ...... 122

We treat our spouses the way the Bible tells us to treat them. ...... 122

The husband recognizes, like Oh my gosh, I am going to walk with my wife in an understanding way. I am going to show her that I understand her. I am going to work to teach her and love her....... 123

We are supposed to look at the world; we do not look at it through just our own opinions or even through just our own experiences. 124

Believers, you know, so the point is not just to have a comfortable, happy marriage, the point is to be holy, and the point is the salvation of your spouse's soul is the most important thing. ...... 124

It's true that Jesus came to save us. He reconciles us with the father so we can have a great relationship with him. Without Jesus, we can't save ourselves. ...... 125

You should believe today that you love so much that they would share the gospel that they want you to be saved. ...... 125

Rejoice in persecution. People who believe in Jesus rejoice because of the hope they have and so, like I said, this gospel is not just that we would have a happy, comfortable life now, but that we have eternal hope in Jesus Christ. ...... 126

What fellowship does light have with darkness? ...... 126

Working in the same direction. ...... 127

Going to church does not mean being a Christian. ...... 128

To be married less will be called singleness more will be called to marriage, so marriage is right. ...... 128

How do you know if you, as a wife, will save your husband, or how do you know if you, as a husband, will save your wife? ...... 129

The Bible advises against divorcing an unequally yoked spouse. Once you make a covenant commitment with someone, God wants you to honor that commitment and avoid divorce. ...... 129

You need to stay married ...... 130

Paul is giving advice on how to handle that ...... 130

The Bible will never contradict itself ...... 131

You are going to want to resolve in your heart to put God first no matter what you do ........ 132

I also believe dating a non-believer is unbiblical ........ 132

Live in a Biblical relationship ........ 134

Like the way you can guard your heart when you are doing these other things ........ 134

You should be a witness to this person who does not know Christ135

Way to guard your heart; The fourth thing that you can do when you have feelings for this person. ........ 135

God's word by becoming unequally yoked and not obeying God, hoping that this person one day obeys God ........ 136

The way that you go about interacting with the world will figure out if you are going to get pulled down or pulled up. ........ 136

Do not get pulled down like that ........ 137

Brothers! If anyone is caught in any transgression, you who are spiritual should restore him in a spirit of gentleness ........ 138

Guarding your heart well ........ 138

You are going to, you know, start dating them and turn your back on God for this relationship ........ 139

If they become a Christian, they start bearing the fruits of the spirit ........ 139

There is something with you that I hope could encourage you a little bit ........ 140

God helped me to see much relief ........ 140

Christians believe that divorce is not something that you should do ........ 141

When it not sinful to be divorced ........ 141

Yet realize the difference between a false disciple and a true disciple ........ 142

Miraculously God saved their marriage ........ 143

In times of trouble, a Leader, pastor, Doctor, or marriage counselor is important. ........ 144

God hates divorce. ........ 144

Let man not separate what God has joined together ...................... 145

I endured suffering and bore some of the extra sufferings of Christ in my body ........................................................................................ 146

God is saying to you let go of what is dead ................................. 146

You cannot love your loved ones (Father, Mother, Wife and children, Brother, and sister) more than God................................ 147

Above all things, guard your heart............................................... 148

God's vengeance is overcoming evil not by being overcome by evil but by overcoming evil with good. Be Christ-like and be willing to suffer ........................................................................................... 149

Just know you have a brother in Christ who is praying for you .... 149

God's word is remarkably interesting. We have so much to say about this subject; An unbeliever with a believer is a big responsibility 150

As the Bible says that the unbeliever is free to live, and so it is not a problem for that person to remarry because if the person marries and leave ............................................................................................ 150

I want people to understand everyone needs Jesus ....................... 151

Believe in Jesus; he is the only one who is going to wash away your sins ............................................................................................. 151

Believing in Jesus is the only way you are going to wash away your sins ............................................................................................. 152

True Christian, a true believer; You love God, you accepted Jesus in your life........................................................................................ 152

There is grace in Jesus's name .................................................... 153

They do everything possible to solve the situation. If it is something that cannot be solved, then God knows everything. We are not going to be the ones that tell God what to do ......................................... 154

Basically, what he is saying here is that I am giving you a new fresh command from God ...................................................................... 154

He is simply saying I am giving you something that Jesus has not previously mentioned.................................................................... 155

He is simply saying I am giving you something that Jesus has not previously mentioned.................................................................... 156

Otherwise, your children would be unclean, but as it is, they are holy ..................................................................................................... 156

The word "sanctified" means set apart, and the word "holy" means set apart ........ 157

If the unbeliever leaves, let it be so the brother or the sister is not bound in such circumstances. God has called us to live in peace.. 158

Most scholars will interpret that and say, "That means that you are now free to marry someone else if they are a believer." ........ 158

Many times, people will have this newfound relationship with Christ, and they will neglect their responsibilities to their spouse 159

Against your morality, that goes against your integrity, that goes against some of the things that you believe as a Christian. Remember, the order of submission is always God first. ........ 159

Never give up on the power of prayer if you are married to an unbeliever ........ 160

Whenever you are being mistreated by your spouse, you want to respond in such a way that your spouse is left saying, "Wow! the way I treated her the way that I treated him deserves this type of response ........ 160

The more we may be pushing them away and not allowing God to do the work in their life ........ 161

What I have seen repeatedly is that when the husband is not a believer, the woman tends to stunt her spiritual role because she follows or gives in to his leadership ........ 162

Your desire to get involved in church and the history of your small groups and hang out with all your Christian friends is now taking you further ........ 162

Further away from your family responsibilities. Remember that you still have a major obligation as a husband and as a wife ........ 163

Further away from your family responsibilities, remember that you still have a major obligation as a husband or as a wife ........ 164

Adam and Eve by saying. God's holding out on you. This command where he said, "Do not eat of this tree," is because he is holding out on you, and it is better for you to disobey God. Obey him ........ 165

Because we were raised in this environment. ........ 165

Do not yoke yourself with somebody who is not trying to please God ........ 166

Now you cannot have a romantic relationship where you are not giving and taking. ........ 167

Now you cannot have a romantic relationship where you are not giving and taking ........ 167

Do not live your life in a completely unique way........ 168

As a Christian with a biblical worldview, marriage has a very specific meaning. It is one of the highest representations of how Christ and the church love one another. ........ 169

What we have produced help for marriage, it differentiate us from everyone else........ 169

A body and a mind is what we need. ........ 170

What they are doing, or you could use this as a thread to go into your own mind. ........ 171

Prayer for any situation you're in now in your married life........ 171

For Adam, there was not found a helpmate who fit perfectly with him. ........ 172

Not everyone is going to see a vision of his wife. ........ 173

You must contribute to the kingdom of God. ........ 173

Take your responsibilities. ........ 174

It is going to be good for everyone to have knowledge about this book. ........ 175

The prophetic clear means either prophecy or the ministry of the Holy Spirit in your life. ........ 175

It must be handled with maturity because marriage is a great issue. Are you getting my ........ 176

People engage in all kinds of skills and spiritual activities in their bid to recover back the Kingdom. ........ 176

Marriage and prophecy. ........ 177

It was God himself that appointed Saul to be king. He can do the same for your marriage. ........ 177

In a guided atmosphere of the world and spiritual maturity, prophecy can be enormously powerful. Hallelujah! ........ 178

Do not be a dead person in the house of God. ........ 178

The Bible said he broke bread, and their eyes were open........ 179

Your spouse needs to be pleased with your marriage. 180
I know this might sound very sciency but let me explain briefly .. 180
Do not get into arguments 181
Unhappiness can make the marriage suffer 181
What to avoid in other for your marriage to stay healthy and happy 181
Your spouse's demand is particularly important 182
Because it can help you save your marriage 182
Talking through issues tends to simply reinforce your spouse's belief that the marriage does indeed have real problems 183
It might take weeks or even months to make progress, especially if you are only seeing therapists 184
It now with rebuilding a broken marriage is a rocky broke sometimes; things can get worse before they get better 184
Do not feel desperate 185
Be polite, and you will resolve this issue 186
Get control of your emotions 186
Do not be depressed 187
Outline the mistakes 187
Holy Spirit comes into our marriage 188
Do not poison the marriage. It is created by God in the Garden of Eden 188
They are going to find out what to do to save their marriage 189
You, your Marriage, and your family in God's side 190
They are going to fight to save their marriage because marriage has never been something that was easy from the ancient time to the present moment 190
A marriage that has money is a marriage where they are going to know some exceptionally good days, some joyful days 191
We are living in a time where sometimes, even though you do everything by yourself on your own, that does not mean you are going to have the outcome that you wanted 191
Prayer for Individuals in marriage 192

Bibliography ........................................................................ 193
Do not live according to the flesh ................................................ 193
Renew your mind, do not live by the flesh .................................... 194
If anyone is in Christ, he is a new creation .................................... 195
Roman 12:2 ........................................................................ 195

# Introduction

I'm writing this book because I see it in the society we are living in today. Marriage is losing its essence; people tend to get married for any reason they want and divorce for no reason at all. That is not what the Bible talks about. Because it says that some people are great Christians and they live the kind of marriage they should live according to the Bible's principles. But in general, people can see that marriage principles are not respected throughout the world.

There are many reasons why we talk about marriage in this book because Marriage is created by God. Marriage is a mystery of faithful love in God, in the book of Genesis 2:18-25. The Lord God called Adam to name all the animals that living creatures feature Adam no suitable helper was first found for it or Adam's helper was first found in verse 21, do not cut cause men to fall all into a deep sleep and why while he was sleeping and then close it says, because it is not good for man to be alone, there was a need why God created the woman that's name is Eve. She was created to complete Adam's needs, Adam was alone and incomplete. God as a provider, saw Adam's need, He created Eve to complete him. Adam loves her and said, "You are flesh of my flesh, bones of my bones, I will call you "woman" because you are from a man.

Marriage is not a game that people play when they want.

It is an institution that God created.

# You, your marriage, and your family in God's side

Corinthians:12:16

12: To the rest, I say this (I, not the Lord): if any Man has a wife who is not a believer and if she is willing to live with him, he must not divorce her.

13: And if a woman has a husband who is not a believer and she is willing to live with him, she must not divorce him,

14: for the unbelieving husband has been sanctified through his wife, and the unbelieving wife has been sanctified through her believing husband otherwise, the children would be unclean but as it is they are holy.

15: but if the unbeliever leaves let him do so a believing man or woman is not bound in such circumstances. God has called us to live in peace

16: how do you know wife whether you will save your husband or how do you know husband whether you will save your wife.

## The spirituality of the Church

Corinth, in the ancient world, was considered a bad city according to its lifestyle. They even created a verb for the Corinthians, "Christianize," which means "to live without shame and in immorality." For these reasons, Corinth was on the list of cities where it was difficult to convert to the Christian faith. But the apostle Paul worked in Corinth for 18 months (about one and a half years). It was a surprise for all that the Church he founded became one of the greatest ones in the 1st century. Many years later, Paul learned that the faithful Church was ruined by spiritual sickness, which is why he wrote this letter in which Paul gave them some practical advice for those problems in the Church, and he encouraged the Corinthians to live like the first Christians that one of the greatest issues that Paul talked about in first Corinthians 7:12-16 which is "the problems of married people." That is what we are going to talk about when a Christian could divorce her or his spouse.

## How to live your marriage in difficult circumstances (times)?

Paul wrote in 1 Corinthians in Ephesus on his third missionary journey. We see that in Acts 19:1 and 1 Corinthians 16:8,9. In 56 or 57 AD, Paul had previously written a letter to the Corinthians that has not come down to us, and in that letter, he had warned them against associating with immoral people according to his first missionary Journey. In verse 59, Paul received a letter in which they declared it was impossible to follow his advice without going out of the wall altogether and gave him a number of problems on which they asked his opinion. This letter from the covenant was brought by three of their members, Stephans, Fortunatis, and Achaius, who came to visit Paul at Ephesus and undoubtedly told him about the conditions of the Church from the servant of Chloe these problems caused him pain and anxiety.

## Your marriage and the culture

Corinth is a city in Greece on the narrow isthmus between the Peloponnesus, Athens was still the educational center of Greece, but Corinth was the capital of the Roman province they call Achaia and are the most of the commercial between Rome, and the east was brought to its harbors. Corinth occupied a strategic geographical position. It was situated at the southern extremity of the isthmus, at the northern foot of the lofty. Corinth had an ancient and remarkably interesting history. They introduced so many gods, like Poseidon, the god of the sea, and Aphrodite, the goddess of love. Her temple on Acro Corinth had more than 1000 hierodule Priestesses of vice. Corinth was a city of wealth for much traffic through commerce. Corinth made a lot of money. Corinth had many industries. In Paul's days, the population of Corinth had been estimated at about 200,000 free people in addition to a half million slaves. And some rich ones.

## Couples living next to strangers

They received many strangers for many reasons the nearby city of Athens and Achaia, and Delphi. The term epistle is, however, a technical one referring particularly to the 21 epistles of the New Testament. The epistle was written to individual churches or groups of churches.

## According to the Bible, Christians should never be divided among themself (keep the Marriage Holy)

In the first letter to the Corinthians, apostle Paul talked about many repeated things. We think that the most important thing might be divisions. The first goal of Paul here is to tell the Corinthians that they should not be divided as Christ is not divided to God or to himself. They should love one another and be in a perfect union; the passage that we are studying has a major section with instructions on marriage and a minor section. Paul is writing about the problems of marriage.

People, there are some words, like in verse 14, that shows the consequence of any woman who has a husband who is an unbeliever, and he consents to live with her; she should not divorce him because the unbelieving husband is made holy through her. We also have verse 15, which shows a contrast between the unbeliever who wants to leave and let him do so. We can consider other verses like 2 Corinthian 12:17 and Roman.14:19 to support Paul's idea.

## The responsibility of the believer in the Marriage

The word (Alpha phi, I'N'Mi) is the most important in 1 Corinthians 7:12-16, and it is one of the more frequent words in this passage. It helps to understand the passage better. However, this word could have other meanings. It is repeated more than two times by the author in this passage. Paul writes this word in an infinitive, "Alphie," which means "to send off," and it is richly attested in Greek from a preliminary period. It was used in every nuance, both literal and figurative, from to hurt to release, to let go or to let be Ephesians, pina to release someone from a legal relation, whether office, Marriage, obligation, or debt, though never in a religious sense. Paul uses these words to a couple that is already married when one of them becomes a Christian, if, at all possible, they should remain together, unless the unbeliever, whether the person refuses to remain or wants to leave the Marriage.

## God wants his people to live in peace

In first Corinthians 7:12-16, one of the most common and most important words could be "des." It helps to have a better view of the passage. In fact, many Bible translators translate it as "to bind." It is common in the New Testament, in the same sense of "to bind" or "to bend together," "to bind to," and most often "to chain." This can easily pass over into the sense of imprisonment, and it can be used for the mutual commitment of partners in marriage. Paul said that the believer is not under obligation to try to continue living with the unbeliever because God wants his people to live in peace. If the unbeliever were forced to live with the believer, there would be no peace in the home. (Theological Dictionary of the New Testament, page 60).

## Return to the ancient love (the first Gospel)

Finally, Paul was personally concerned with the Corinthians' problems revealing a true Bishop's (pastor's Doctor's) heart. He tries to correct the Corinthians' conduct in the church. He wanted that they return as they used to be in the past. The Church in Corinth was a surprise for all and the 1st century.

## Your marriage needs to be a model to the Pagans

No one thought that the Corinthians would convert to the Christian faith with their bad reputation because many terrible things happened there at that very moment. The Christians imitated the pagans' behavior and gave problems in the Church. Paul wanted that they serve as a model to the pagans instead of doing sad things and especially to those who were married, he wanted them to remain with their spouse if they were willing to live even if they were not Christians, but if the non-Christians refused to live let him or her do so. Today we as Christians need to make good decisions in a way to please God. We cannot today leave our wives or husbands for any reason. As Christians, we need to suffer or be patient to reach people to Christ, so the unbelieving one is sanctified to the believer, and the children are holy.

## Bibliography

The new international study Bible Theological Dictionary of the New Testament volume second edited by G Kittel theological revised King James GD Douglas the new international Dictionary of the Bible's grand rapid Michigan Zondervan publishing 1987 Edward W Goodrich and John R call and burger to eat the NIV exhaustive concordance grand rapid Michigan 49530 Zondervan publishing in 1990 praise the Lord.

Now, I'm going to start with weddings and Ephesians 5 verses 20-22.

*"Wives, submit to your husband as to the Lord, for the husband is the head of the wife as Christ is the head of the church. His body, of which you receive, you know what I did the in the church so submit to Christ so also wives should submit to their husbands and everything."*

## Husband, love your wives as Christ loved the Church

Husband, love your wife's life just as Christ loves the church,and he gives himself up for it. The firstborn was holy, by the blood of

Jesus, and presented her to himself the church without wrinkle or any other blemish but as holy and blessed and this same way, Be holy. Those who love their wives as their own bodies, he who loves his wife loves himself. After all, no one ever hated his own body, but he feeds and cares for it, just as Christ does for the church, for we are members of his body. For this reason, a man will leave his father and mother and be united with his wife, and the two will become one flesh. This is a story, but I am talking about Christ and the church. However, each one of you also must love his wife as he loves him himself, and the wife must respect her husband. Today I am incredibly happy to be able to talk about marriage as we started, we see, Paul said in Ephesians.

## A marriage ceremony is a victory for the couple in our society today

Marriage, which is not something that we found in the community today, Marriage, is an institution that God created. It is going to enforce the church, even on those that know it, in every detail. This is a victory in our society today when someone is getting married. From marriage, we find a family with the birth of children, and with a lot of family that create a better society. When the unbelieving wife or unbelieving husband is married to a believer, what we wanted to let you know in this book is that. We want to let you know that when two people marry, like a man marries a woman, and they both are Christians, this is the perfect union because if both are Christians. The Bible says when you know the word of God, you live a better married life. A perfect marriage does not mean that they will never have any problems, but how they will deal with that problem, but they are going to know how to solve the problem because they are Christian. The Bible itself tells us about how to resolve those issues.

## Why it is important to respect your husband

That happens in marriages today. It is saying one thing that I want to say about why it is important to respect your husband. This is what He says to the wife in the Bible as the ladies need to respect their husbands, and He asked the man to love the ladies that are our wives. What does that mean if the lady respects the man, there will be no problem.

## Choose your partner according to your faith in God. Your spouse is for life

If the husband loves his wife, there will be no problem, but today in our society, they teach something different; they have something different when they make sure they talk about you. You need to know where the men that there is no such thing anymore that to me everyone wants to do whatever they want, especially according to their needs because some people, they may marry the men married to women, but when they find a different person tell him how to live especially in those days. We see in our society that people tell us that if you are a lady and you went to school, maybe you study the law or something else like photography or Medicine or else. You said that you are a physician, and then they are going to say OK. The lady did not have enough time to go to school; now is the time, whatever it is, to go to school, stuff like that. And then talk about how to share their deal with responsibility about taking care of kids, taking care of the home, and the last thing that becomes the most important thing in the marriage.

## It is not really my viewpoint, but it is according to the Bible

Which issues to study today because there is something called competition people going to try to say who is the best who is the better? I am talking about marriage today. I am not talking about those people because I say. I am going to repeat that the only places you are going to find my marriage is in the Bible, and God is the one that started the marriage, and I am not talking; I am going to talk about this specific person, but what I am doing in my life. If I say my viewpoint if it is not really my viewpoint, but it is according to the Bible. What I am saying here is not my word, but it's how the Bible sees that. Wait, and see what is happening in this society today because today, people who claim to be married do not even do the union that they have because people married if you are willingly married according to the Bible, you are going to have an exceptionally good life in the marriage but if you live like you marry because you see a friend of yours getting married, it is not genuinely nice. A man who praise them to say congratulation because they are getting married, they have exceptionally beautiful stuff like you going to let us see one. Wow! Men and women get married at age 22, but this is what it is; marriage is something more important than seeing something that you want to do. And then people today may become a burden for them because of finances because they need a man with a lot of money.

They need a lady that has a lot of money; if the lady does not have enough money, they are going to go away because he does not have enough money. They are going to go away because those who are not going to live with one another have to be patient to work together to make things work perfectly for both.

## Marriage is instituted by God. Genesis 2:18-25

Because she was taken out of a man for this cause, a man shall leave his father and his mother and she'll leave to be his wife and they shall become one flesh and the man and his wife were both naked and were not ashamed some of you made the mistake giving your children the Christmas gift printed on the outside of the box the words some assembly required about 1% of you probably got out the instruction sheet read it through from start to finish as they say you should before beginning the project and put it together that way but the rest of you probably thought well I'm you know this and you got out of your tools and started in and you got a ways into it and discovered that you needed to go back and read those instructions marriage comes with a label on the box that says much assembly required in fact it takes an entire lifetime to put together a marriage but probably like most of the parents who got those kind of gifts for their kids this Christmas if you're like most of us you sort of plunged into marriage 19 handle it

## God's design for Christian marriage

I can figure it out as we go, and you started trying to put together the parts as you figured it, and you got into trouble and at some point needed to get out and read and reread and probably reread the instruction manual and most of the problems we get into in marriage can be traced to our lack of following what God has written about the subject early in this book of beginnings. In the book of Genesis, we find God's design for Christian marriage, and this text describes the original marriage as the basis for almost everything else that the Bible says about the subject of marriage. It builds on this text in one way or another, it explains for us God's reason for marriage and shows us many principles that apply to the institution of marriage, and we will be blessed, and we will be a blessing to others and have marriages that honor God if we follow His instruction manual, in a nutshell, our text is teaching us that God designed marriage to meet our need for companionship and also to provide an illustration of our relationship with God.

## God's personal relationship with the creation

And through that illustration, of course, God wants to be honored and glorified as He shines through in our home, life, and the world in which we live. There's interesting that in Genesis chapter one, the name that is used for God is the Hebrew Elohim which is the name of God in his power; in chapter 2 consistently, the name used for bodies and getaways translated in my Bible as Lord in capital small capital the Lord God that emphasizes God's personal relationship with his creation God is the covenant and critics, of course, say these come from two separate stories that were pieced together, the author knew what he was doing, and He's trying to show us that the powerful creator God is also personal God who cares for His creation and who meets their every need as He is here meeting Adam's need for a helper a partner for him and

## A contrast, (It is not good and it is good)

So God here takes action to meet Adam's need for companionship which is one of the main for marriage do you're reading through the text if you'd started at and this is 11 it just kept reading on through and you came to chapter two verse 18 it kind of charges at you or it hits you abruptly because no less than six times in chapter one verse 10:12: 18: 21: 25 and 31 it says the Lord saw His creation and it was good and it was good and it was good and this is repeated over and over again and then you get to chapter two verse 18 and it says the Lord watch said it is not good, this is contrast this is different, one is not good it is not good for the man to be alone and that's quite a statement if you stop and think about it here you have a man who has never seen Maine as God's creature put on the earth in the garden of Eden in a perfect environment there is nothing that has tainted the earth at this point the man is as in as close a relationship with the living God as any creature could be and yet God says.

## Marriage is instituted by God. Genesis 2:18-25

It is not good that he should be alone that's significant you know sometimes I think super spiritual people will tell you if you feel lonely especially if you're single well just trust the Lord you know if you just trust the Lord more you wouldn't be lonely when you used to tell me that when I was single I used to wait a minute that isn't biblical because God said right here to Adam's perfect fellowship with him in a perfect environment it's good for that man to be alone now that is not to say that every person is to be married obviously all of us are single for a good part of our life usually at least the 1st 20 years sometimes longer and sometimes if we lose a maiden in doubt that the tail end for a number of years besides that God has called some to be single and besides all of that marriage doesn't meet all our needs from companionship we need one another we need relationships with friends of the same sex even when we're married but it is to say this a main reason that God designed the marriage relationship was for that need of companionship.

## God's direction on marriage

It was not met even by fellowship with the Lord's self and that is a significant right we have to understand what to come to the subject of marriage that God designed it is not the human evolutionary sociological product of societies and all of this stuff that we're bad in the university's marriage was designed originally and given to us by God and God understands how it operates and God has given us direction on it in His word and that means that it takes 3 for a marriage a good marriage not just the husband and the wife but it takes God and God should be at the center of every marriage and that means that for a Christian to marry an uncle is to enter into marriage like with one leg cut off you you're just hobbling along and it's never going to be all that God designed it to be because God has to be at the center of that marriage someone has described marriage as a triangle with God at the apex and the husband and wife at the other corners the closer that both partners draw to the Lord the closer they draw to one another and the reverse is true the further they go from the Lord the further they are from one another and we see that even here because.

## Marriage in the Garden of Eden

After Adam and Eve disobeyed God, there was alienation between them, and in chapter three, we see Adam beginning to blame Eve for his problems, and we've been with that game ever since, so you know it's her fault his 12, and then we see the couple immediately beginning to hide themselves from not only God but from one another by the fig leaves and so on and so the starting place in other words of having a godly marriage is each partner needs to be genuinely converted to the Lord Jesus Christ and then they each need a daily walk with him so that they are growing progressively close to the Lord and it's safe to say that every time a marriage breaks down one or both partners have walked away from the Lord or

## Feminism does not let ladies be a helper

They're drifting from God's marriage and must be centered on Him. Now God says here that He will make a helper suitable for Adam and that Hebrew word is not a demeaning word; in fact, it is one used by God himself in other parts of scripture to show that He is our helper refused of military assistance, and it points to the fact that the husband needs his wife and depends upon her and needs her support and help at the same time we need to keep in mind in this day of the so-called feminism first Corinthians 11-9 where the apostle Paul says the man was not made for the woman's sake but the woman was made for the man's sake I know of so-called evangelical leaders were the wife is a pastor and the husband kind of follow her around in her career as.

## Preach salvation in your marriage

If it doesn't matter, it's all egalitarian that one verse refutes where Paul says that it's backward the woman was made for the man's sake and not vice versa; now he's quick to point out, though, that we need each other, and so there is no superiority of or anything like that on the man it is just creation, and then the order is that we should reflect the divine image and the divine image Jesus Christ is eternally subject to the father he was subject to before the world was created because we know that the Lamb of God was given to him given his life even before as Jesus submitted to the God for our redemption he submitted to the father and taking on human flesh and going on to the cross Paul says that in eternity future Jesus will render up the Kingdom to the father and all things will be in him and so for eternity the sons committed to the father in order to carry out the divine plan and in the same way husband and wife were to work together in equality and

## Feminism destroys Marriage in the 21st century

Yet in order to submit the wife so that they can function as a picture of the divine image and feminism destroys that, it is very it's not too strong to say it is satanic at its core because Satan was the one who came and tempted Eve and awarded the divine purpose right at the start and by the way too Adam's leadership of his wife is seen here before the fall in naming her names her in verse 23 and as I said it if you have the authority to name then you are responsible over something and so that is seen right here, and we'll go into that more next week in Ephesians chapter 5, but God makes this helper for Adam.

## Equality in marriage but distinct roles to fulfill

But it doesn't mean again that Adam is superior, and the word corresponds to it like a jigsaw puzzle where it's not all there; you don't have all the parts, you can't get the full picture, and we need one another in Christian marriage, and the man needs the woman, the woman needs the man they're both equal in personhood, equal before God and yet have distinct roles to fulfill, now the dust chapter 2 verse seven you have to ask as you read the story why didn't God make Eve from the dust, why did He make her from Adam's rib as we read, I believe that part of the answer there is that God was trying to show Adam that his wife was not lower than him in any way.

## The husband must treat his wife as his own body

But she was very part of him as Adam exclaims, "...bone of my bones, the flesh of my flesh." Paul picks up on that and says the wife is like the husband's own body. It's part of him; he is to nourish and cherish her, treat her tenderly, as Christ does the church. Someone has observed that Eve was not taken from Adam's head that she should rule over him, nor was she taken from his feet that he should rule over her in that sense, but she was taken from his side that he might protect her and hold her close to his heart and it seems out of context of asking

Adam to name the animals in verses 19 and 20. Liberal critics say it is out of context; I contend it's right there for a purpose, and the purpose is that God wanted Adam to sense his need for a wife before he gave her to him, He had him named the animals now Adam learned a lesson as he names the animals.

## In marriage, the wife fulfills the husband's needs in all

I know he wasn't speaking English, but I assume he started with art bark and worked his way through to zebra you know, by the time he got part way through the alphabet, he's beginning to, and then he gets to himself, and the forlorn message at the end of verse 20 is but for Adam there was not found a helper suitable for him he's all alone, and so I believe that God made Adam feel the need for a wife, and then he met the needs so that Adam would appreciate what God had done I don't relate to it I suppose as much as Adam, but I know when I was about 20 I wanted to be married and God helped me fulfill, I was almost 27 and I now knew my need when I was 20 but by the time I was 27 I really knew my need and that made me really appreciate my wife and I want to say I still do 21 years ago last week there we met and I really do appreciate her and thank God for her but God is that way he lets us know our need and sometimes strings us out quite a while to let us know our need and then he meets that need and we can thank him for it by the way men who haven't told your wife you appreciate her lately.

# A gift from God that the husband needs to appreciate

I hope you do so not just as a response to this but as a habit to let her know how God has given her to you and how much you appreciate her. This account of this first marriage plainly, straightforwardly, and without embarrassment shows that God designed the sexual response or relationship in the marriage. We see evidence of this in the mention of becoming one flesh in verse 24 and the lack of shame in the nudity of the man and his wife in verse 25. Christians sometimes get ashamed of sex, even in marriage, and that is not God's way. Some think sex was the original sin; it was not. I once heard about the pastor who told his congregation that he and his wife were going to adopt their first child, Some dear old lady in the church came up to him at the door after and said; "I just think that's wonderful, that's how every pastor ought to have children, and she didn't have God's perspective on that." I'm afraid nothing wrong with adopting, but back in Jonathan Edward's day, this was Puritan America's colonial America. They had the mistaken notion that the day a child was born was identical to the day of the week in which the child had been conceived. That isn't true, of course, but they thought that the funny thing is that dear old puritan Jonathan Edwards had about 10 or 11 kids, and most of them were born on Sunday, so guess what the congregation thought he was doing after church.

God fashioned a woman from a man.

I don't know if you've ever thought much about Genesis 2 here and what picture it presents, but it might surprise you a little bit.

Genesis 2:22 says that God uses a rib taken from Adam to fashion a woman. The word fashioned is the word to build, and the picture is of a sculptor or an artist who is building something, maybe some model out of clay or a sculpture out of wood or something. And since she was built by God, I think you can safely assume eve was well-built, and I think you're going to assume that from Adam's response when he sees her. But interestingly, he didn't just wake up from his nap, and Eve was lying next to him. It says God brought her to the man, and it must have been an interesting experience. I can picture Adam lying there trying to figure out that he feels different and counting his ribs. The Lord then says, Adam, you forgot to name one. He looks up, and there is Eve, not in a wedding dress, of course, but verse 25 makes it clear she was in her altogether, and Adam responds appropriately. Now, this is one of the worst translations, and I looked up every Bible, King James, and James and NIV, and none of them get to verse 23; this is now a good time.

## The first man on the face of the earth, as he sees his wife

*I have found her, He said.*

It sounds like the guys in an anatomy course, you know. The literal Hebrew could easily be given as Yashwa. I mean, he is excited about this woman, and I am not making this up. I looked this up in Kyle and Delich OK they are about as stodgy German 19th-century commentators as you can find these guys you know Hebrew, Aramaic, all these languages, and here is what they said they translated this time! And, they say, it's expressive of joyous astonishment. I mean, here is a guy going wow, as he looks at this beautiful creature that God has brought to him. Just to check, I looked it up in another Victorian commentary, Jamison Faucet Brown, written in that same era. And they say that it is emphatic that it means now, at last, this is the very thing that hits the mark; this is what is desired, their translation of it. So, Adam is excited and remembers these are the first recorded words of the first man on the face of the earth as he sees his wife and goes, wow, you know, it's like Eureka, I have found her, and he is an excited man. So make sure when you read the text you know just downplay it. And then Adam finishes his work of naming the woman and calls her Ishah Hebrew, which comes from the Irish man.

## He cherished her as a very part of himself and saw his wife as God's exquisite gift to him

And shows that he cherished her as a very part of himself and saw his wife as God's exquisite gift to him. Now, these verses teach us something about God. And that is that God is not opposed to our enjoyment of the physical relationship of marriage. Sometimes I think as American Christians, we've listened to the enemy because Satan wants to malign God. And say God doesn't want you to enjoy life. He doesn't want you to have fun and sex. Well, you might have to do it sometimes, don't enjoy it, or that might be a sin. God gave it as a gift in marriage to be esteemed and honored. When you take God's gift out of that context, then it becomes defiled, and it defiles us and causes all kinds of problems. But within the context of God, if it is good, right, and holy, we can thankfully enjoy God's gift to us in that marriage relationship. Now God designed that marriage relationship in large part to meet our need for companionship. Verse 24 shows us that as most here comments on the story Moses is writing verse and this is not Adam's statement because Adam didn't even know what a father and mother were when he was first created. After all, he didn't have any. This is why Moses explains why God gave marriage for this cause because, in other words of the way.

## God Designed Marriage. Genesis 2:18-25.

God designed marriage from the start. Because of the fact that the woman is created from man's bone and flesh of his flesh, the couple is joined together for this cause. A man and his a man shall leave his father and mother and cleave to his wife. Those two shall become one flesh, and that verse shows that marriage should be a primary, permanent, exclusive, and intimate relationship. First of all, companionship requires that marriage be primary God did not make a father and mother for Adam but a wife, and it is important in a marriage that a couple should be mature enough to leave father and mother so that they can cleave to one another and establish A1 flesh relationship and that means that the marriage relationship is primary not the marriage is a very great institution that God created for men to live a happy life. Instead of people getting pregnant and having children, for me, marriage is an institution. There is preparation to get married. It is not something like today. Marriage is something that is particularly important, as we just said in Corinthians.

# Marriage makes the spouse holy in spite of sexuality

And Ephesians. Marriage is an institution created by God, and for Christians. It has helped the church better when I say it. Helped Christians live better in Christ because when you get married, sexuality is not a sin for you. Those that are not married, they have a sin called fornication. If they go for intercourse, that means they commit a sin. However, if a person is married, engaging in sexuality does not mean they are committing a sin. Marriage plays a particularly significant role in the Christian life because it is.

# Marriage protects Christians against sin

To protect the Christians against sin. There are some people that cannot live without having sexual intercourse. Still, that person needs to get married because if that person is Christian and the nature of that person needs to have a sexual relationship all the time, it means if that person is not married, this is called lust. It is a way of living even though you accepted Jesus Christ, but you are not following him and all the things because you are doing certain things that were not what you must do. You must ask for forgiveness in such a situation, but this is not how we should live. We want to make sure, without getting a lady, getting married, and then the problem is over now, you do not have to ask for forgiveness for lust. This is different.

## Your choice as Christians (Who will be your Spouse?)

When you are getting married to a believer, and two people getting married both are believers, the man needs to love his wife, and the lady must respect his husband, and it will be a perfect union. I am talking about those that are unbelievers. Like if you are a Christian, either man or woman, you marry someone; the Bible already lets us know that we cannot marry someone that is an unbeliever.

## In case you have just converted to the Christian faith

Suppose the believer is a lady married to an unbeliever, which should not be happening. In that case, we must make sure that we marry someone that knows the Gospel, that accepts Christ in their life as Lord and Savior, and that lives in the church; that does not mean they will necessarily be the best partner, but at the same time if we do what the Bible says it is going to be better for us.

## What would you do?

We're not going to feel guilty or ashamed of sin if we do what the Bible tells us to do, and then I'm going to talk about unbeliever; like if someone marries an unbeliever according to what the Bible says, if the unbeliever wants to stay in the marriage the Bible says do not divorce the unbeliever because you are a Christian, you are the one serving God and if the unbeliever in the marriage want to stay because I know someone that was in the church and has a man that is was an unbeliever I don't know if

# Facts about an unbeliever

The man was in the church before and left, but I know she was a very great Christian; she was a Christian who always participated in all the church activities, but the man was not a believer. I do not know if he left the church, but he was not a believer; still, the lady stayed with him. Sometimes the lady asked for prayer because the situation was not that good. The man had a certain type of behavior that was not good for the lady, but she did not divorce him.

**Matt 11: 28 (Give the control of your marriage to the Lord)**

Because he was an unbeliever, the Bible says if the unbeliever wants to leave, the Bible gave Christians the possibility to let the unbeliever leave if he or she really wants to do so because God wants us to live in peace. It says that for either men or women because the reason why the Bible asks us not to divorce unbelieving spouses, as it raises the question of how we will know if we are the ones who will save them. The way you're going to live with your wife, who is an unbeliever, would be like Jesus carrying the cross to Golgotha. That means you have a responsibility that is not quite easy for you to bear. Or to carry because as a Christian, as a believer, you live with an unbeliever. You have the responsibility to live with the unbeliever.

# God wants everyone to be saved, as it says

You are a model for unbelievers and responsible for bringing souls to God since God wants everyone to be saved. God has recommended us to go and preach the Gospel to all nations, as stated in Jn 3;16. Those who have accepted Jesus in their lives should be baptized in the name of Jesus and saved through him. As Christians, we need to work for God in everything we do. We have a responsibility to go out and preach the Gospel and let them know about the sacrifice of Jesus on the cross. How about your spouse, the one you love, care for and cherish, who is inside your house? They should be the first person to whom you preach the Gospel.

## Evangelize your Family

When I want to give a testimony, I remember preaching Gospel to my grandparent as it says in Sp:1: that we shouldn't live and stay next to the people making fun of God or those people you've got. I preached the word to my grandparent, and she accepted Christ in her life. This experience was very important at the time because God wanted us to evangelize and required us to do so. That previous experience was not the only one. We have preached the Gospel to so many people, and a lot of them accepted Christ because I evangelized to them. I want to share with you that whenever I have a conversation with someone, I make sure to present Jesus or the Gospel to them. This used to be my approach, and it means that it is our first responsibility to bring the Gospel to our spouse. If I have my wife and she does not know about the Gospel, this is my responsibility and my action to share the Gospel with her.

## Live by example

The way I behave with my wife, she should see Christ through me. She should see the Bible through me and would accept Christ and follow the Bible also. The world often gives us reason to consider divorcing our wives, but the Bible offers guidance on how to navigate difficult times in marriage regardless of our circumstances. By following the teachings of the Bible, we know what to do, and you are going to experience all wonderful times in your marriage.

## Money and the Marriage

You don't need someone to tell you about sharing the responsibility and the house, sharing the bills sharing everything to have a good marriage. But if we follow the Bible, we know that the Bible has everything about marriage. Don't think there is anything you have to add, as it says in the Bible, to have a better marriage. When giving advice about marriage, make sure that it aligns with Biblical teachings.

## Testimony of a Queen with her husband

My husband is my boss; my husband is #1. My husband tells me, hey, sit down. I will sit down. He tells me, you cannot go out with your friends today. I am not going to go out with my friends. So, I tell women out there you want a man in your life. To be happy, it's important to figure out what makes you happy. My husband does many great things for me, and I do the same for him. I obey, respect, and support my husband as the man that he is. I chose a man I wanted to follow and did anything for him because I loved him. When my husband tells me to jump, I'll jump. Whether he wants to sit down, we'll sit down, you're telling me to go in the room or go up on stage. Anyways, that's a message for everyone out there love and cherish the king in your life.

## It is important to have fun

Being in a relationship with an independent person who can handle their own life can sometimes make some people feel insecure. Like, I want someone that's relying on me all the time, and I want them to feel like they need me, and I think it might be a trap for you if that's what you set yourself up with, so that's what I do, find someone that's emotionally independent, someone that you get along well with, someone that calms you, someone who knows you, that's not going to get bent out of shape about little things and if they do it little de-escalation can kind of get the problem solved and then just have fun you know my wife and

## Maturity in the choice

I have fun, and I think that it's important to pay attention to who you choose to marry. Try to find someone who is emotionally independent and can handle their own responsibilities. This is just one idea about choosing a husband based on real-life experience, although it is not necessarily biblical. But it's something in real life, the way you can choose your wife or the way your wife choose you, but we have a lot of Godly viewpoint about marriage, and I want everyone to follow to have in your life because there are some people that are going to win this book that don't get married yet and some others already get married so this book going to be useful for either you already married or either you not married but whatever it is this book going to be good for you.

## Quality of a good husband (character)

The quality of a good husband in marriage today means you do not want to marry a man who is still trying to be like other people. She should want to marry a man who knows who he is. He knows his self-image. He does not need anyone's approval to feel important. He does not try to be cool. She wants to be with somebody who knows if somebody or anybody is anybody. You want a man whose self-confidence and self-image are in God. God took this man and placed him in the garden of Eden. The word Eden means presents. Please get that book on praise and wish to understand what that word means. Even so, the first thing is the man has a good clear image, so maybe secondly.

## Build up the partnership

He is well in the presence of God. The third important thing about the man is that he was given the first command, which is work, so you want the man who was working and loves to work to meet him working. The fourth thing about a man is in Genesis chapters one and two. You'll find this man in verse 15, where God told him to cultivate. This means you need a man who can cultivate, which means to bring the best start-up, to develop you, and to advance you. Don't marry a man who could improve you. I've met ladies who got a good job, good education, got a nice car, a nice apartment, got their own life going together, and then married their husbands.

## Man's responsibility is not relying on the wife

Watches her television and sleeps in her apartment while she is out to work. That is not a woman, that is a fool. You do not marry a man who decreases your value. You want to marry a guy who will increase and improve your value. Some of you ladies get so desperate because you are 30 you grab anything that comes along in the pants and destroys your quality. (Life the 15th, and this man is Janice; at 2:15) In Genesis 2:15, God told the man to guard the garden, which means a true male is a protector. If a man cannot protect you, he is not deserving to be your husband. A true male protects females; he does not use a strain to abuse them and hurt them and domestically violate them, he does not rape them, he does not harass children or commit incest on his little girl or sodomize his son. That is what a real man does; a real man protects everything under his care.

## A Godly man is a protector

As a matter of fact, the best thing that is supposed to be heard by a man when he comes home is when his wife says daddy's home now, everything's OK. Most people think a challenge should say to her father; that's what a child needs to say. No mother needs to say about her husband; he's going to be the shining armor. Here is my protector. He has arrived. He's a Godly Man; he is a real man who God says, "Do not touch the tree; this is my command." This is found in verse 17 of Genesis 2. In other words, the male was given the word of God, not the female, which means that the male was designed by God to be the head of the house, one who keeps his word, and that means the male was supposed to be the one who knows the word, the commandments of God to communicate to his family.

## A real man knows the Bible

This means a real man knows this book called the Bible back to front. Don't marry a man who can't teach you the word. Some of you are too late. There are men who know the name of everybody on the soccer team but can't list the decisions. They know the score of all last year's games but don't know the chapters in the vodka. They spend hours watching television football but spend no hours in the word of God. That's not a good man to marry. I'm going to preach it, baby man; you got to be like Adam if you want to guarantee a good home.

## Good examples for married people

Marriage is a mosaic built with your spouse; millions of tiny moments that create your love. Each marriage is a commitment, a decision to do all through life that will express your love from the start. Marriages are like fingerprints. Each one is different, and each one is we come to love, not by finding a perfect person but by learning to see the imperfect. The first to apologize is the bravest, the first to forgive is the strongest, and the first to forget is the happiest. Does not make the wheel go round; love is what makes the ride worthwhile. The most successful marriages are those where both husband and wife look to build their self-esteem with the other.

## Do you want a secret about marriage?

The secret of a successful married couple is to be ready to share authentic information on navigating marital issues and the secrets of solving them. This is marriage. Let us meet the couples. Our first couple is a duo who has been together for a decade and are known around their town as the Frais and Bercy R. Then we got Rolph and Telfort, and next, we have Daniel and Nathaniel, who are celebrating two decades of nonstop marital life and next, we have Saintil and Jose, and although, she says, she has turned him down three times they have been married for 32 years. Finally give it up for Karen and Larry, who have been together for 49 years let us get that first. Let me start with the pros; let us start over how you fight fair, how well first you pick your battles; we know how to back off and just go into the other room and let it light.

## The things to talk about in marriage

We would not have made it to 50 years, brother, if we did not discuss the things or we did not keep them a secret. We talk all the time, and I know where I can go. I am well trained after 50 years, you know, where I can go, yes, and she knows the same, so you just worked it for us. I can either be right, or I can be happy; I just take the happy road.

There were times to work for what we did early on in our marriage. We were married for about a year, and we had a pretty big blow-up. That's when we decided that we were setting rules, rule number one, and we still live by today. We do not allow the volume to go past five, so we don't go to six or seven; it stays right at 5. Then we also decided that we would never call each other by their names, so she won't talk about the size of my head, and then we also decided rule number 3, which was that whenever we have a conflict, we would never involve each other's family, so I won't say anything about her mom she won't say anything about my family and after 30 years.

## Not about winning but about God's will

We are still living by those rules of conflict because, for us, you know, it is not about winning an argument; it should not be about winning. It should be about being in God's will, so that is the key to our arguments. I feel the biggest thing with us is that whenever we have an argument, I never mention something that happened from the earlier argument because, obviously, I forget. I do not remember because it just comes in and out, but that is, you know, really the wonderful thing about her. That is one of the reasons why I am married. When we have a conflict, it is like when we get past that. I never repeat, and when I forgive you, it is totally forgotten.

## How to forgive and forget in marriage

I do not even remember it is overnight. A lot of people would do well to service that if you are going to keep bringing up the past, then you did not forget it. And you did not forgive that is right, so now obviously still the problem is so you are supposed to forgive and forget say one more thing though yes, the best thing about arguing though is making up and we make up because it is a good thing.

## The outcome of marriage

Let me ask you, ladies and gentlemen, how did you all have at the beginning of your marriage or about after two years? For us, it was blissful for the first couple of years, we didn't know how much we were going to argue, and we moved to New York City. There was this morning that we had the very first explosive fight of our marriage, and I said you are a lousy husband, he looked at me, and his face just like totally went blank, and he left. Well, normally, we would walk to work together. He left and slammed the door. It's like we were in this walk-up, and it just slammed the whole building when

## Details about disagreements

He slammed the door and left, so I left about 10 minutes later, but right about that time, everybody started running across the street and started screaming. I looked up, and just as I looked up just after, the plane flew into the first tower, and wow! I saw my husband was going downtown. It is the World Trade Center! Oh wow! And so I lived with that for about four or five hours. Is that going to be the last thing that I said to him. and after that, we had some ugly fights because there were issues. But after that, we knew we needed language. We needed a way to disagree with each other, a way to get on the plane, to never say something and leave or go to bed with anger that we're going to regret. Then also because of what she said to me right after that, I get to downtown, the first plane hit, and I'm thinking, you know I'm a lousy husband.

# A husband's behavior in marriage

She does not really need to know that I am okay now but do not do that. Do not call her right away, right? You know man, what I have gathered from this question right here is really I am the one at the argument with my voice going up first. I am first, and Marjorie will go, "Wait, excuse me, excuse me, why are you raising your voice," and then I got the herald pumped down. I got the hair cause if I keep this tone at this level up here, I will come back speed, you know, because she just gives me the silent treatment; I cannot stand that; she walked around the house for four hours and

# Better communication in the marriage

I have been worse. The treatment was the worst; I am not it, fellas. It is the worst when your wife is not speaking to you. Hey man, do not do that, you should be sitting up, man, and always ease on in that baby. Let me tell you what I was trying to say, it's hard to get back, primarily a long time, but we have an agreement; it is that we will never go to bed, man. That's right; we'll work it out. Now let me tell you something; try to live by that, don't go to bed mad because I got news. If you go to bed mad, you are going to wake up and be okay, but when she wakes up, and she is mad up there she was last night because she didn't think of some more stuff, you are the world of trouble there what's the biggest mistake that most people make before they say I do, I got this one Caprice and Ronald a lot of people say, I do but what they really mean is I'll try, before they get married, they did not get full disclosure.

Saying you know separation, I do not get that when you say to me, you are going to do whatever you were doing. What I'm going to do, is what you do too, so you got to make sure you say I do to something that you know. You can live with thinking that you can change somebody's thinking, that you can change them, things will get better, and you can't go in with an agenda. I think one of the big mistakes that a lot of people make is before they get married, they don't get full disclosure. I think before you get married, you ought to put everything on the table, no secrets, let them know your credit report, let him know, let him know everything. I mean no secrets because that can ruin the marriage. Now, we have been married for 30 years, and I have seen people who never get to this point here because something popped up in year number 10 that a person did not know, and if they had known before, they would not have never said, "I do." They would have said, "I do not."

## See yourself in the mirror

And so, it is best to let everything out before you say, "I do," and if they can marry you with all your info, it's going to be okay. I can see that, but James has been married for almost 49 years, and we still are finding common ground if we can find it, and we very seldom ever argue about anything; I just trained myself well or what, but we just don't have any conflicts. Our biggest argument is over the dishwasher. This man has always helped me so much in the house, and he helps me unload the dishwasher if he's handy, and then he'll load the dishwasher, and it's like he's never seen the dishwasher before. This is where a lot of people are having problems in marriage today. The heaviest problem in marriage today shows how they share their lives together, how they perceive life, and how they communicate with other.

We have a lot of testimony today about marriage's environment. People, how they see neighbors, even sometimes the place they live, the environment, all these things are factors that affect marriage today, so I am incredibly happy to have all these testimonies. We have a lot of testimony today about marriage that we want to encourage people. We are going to develop those ideas because some problems that couples consider as the problem are not really a problem. Those are the reasons.

## The foundation of marriage

We want to make sure we stay on the bible is that it tells us what to do. There are some people that talk about how they are going to handle the problem, as they put them on paper some people put them on paper to know. "Do not call him," "what about the sheep of his head," "do not tell her about his weight," "how tall he is." All these things are things that before marriage they can talk about and [again incomplete]

## The Marriage from the Bible

See if that person is a good fit before because, as Christians, this book is for Christians. When I say for Christians, everybody can read it, but it's going to be in a religious book, it's not going to be a book that we're going to add into everything, even though we have something, we're going to try to edit this information to make sure we take out everything that is not from the bible. We might have some ideas from everyday life, but they are not going to be the main idea; they're not going to be even the supportive idea.

## Commitment is what bound the partners in marriage

They are just going to be there to help you understand the reality that the author is explaining to you in this book because this book is about salvation. How can you solve a problem in your marriage? How can you save your husband if he is an unbeliever? How can you save your wife if she is an unbeliever? That is the main importance of this book, and the other thing we want to make sure we talk about in this book is making sure we encourage people to get married because marriage is an exceptionally good institution for those who serve God. It's an exceptionally good institution that encourages people because this is a way of life that is going to make life better for you, for your partner, for your children, and for generations to come. That is the reason we want to write this book because the bible already tells us what to do.

## Do not doubt yourself if your marriage is not working

If we are really going to see all those people that have good habits, they will say that those ideas came from the Bible. Those people who follow the bible, the ones that are going to have a successful marriage, let me tell you something. Don't say you are not a Christian. If the devil attacks you in your marriage, don't say you are not a Christian because you have problems in your marriage; sometimes you can do the best you can, but that doesn't mean the man or woman is going to be good for you.

## The effective way of living with your spouse

This is because there can be some problems in the marriage, but I am encouraging people to follow the bible's steps. If you go to Corinthians, you will find in this book, if you go to Ephesians, and I am going to give you some other places in the bible, like Genesis, to go to find the effective way of living with your spouse, that is going to be the best thing to do everything else can be added as an example.

## It is Good

The main goal, the title, and the subject are in the bible. This is what we want to talk about today because we are giving you a practical book, not only a written book, but we want to give you a practical book. Something that is useful, we will practice with some people that have been married for like 50 years ago and with those who have been married ten years ago, twenty years ago, thirty years ago. They keep living in the marriage, and they can talk about it. Those are real-life stories, and those are the things we want to talk about in this book. There is a right way to the dishwasher, it is my way, and it is the right way, trust me. I can come to your house and teach you. Honora, and Telfort, what is the biggest mistake you think people make before they get married.

## Effective communication skills.

You have to say what you want before you get married. I think the biggest mistake that a lot of couples have been doing is that they keep bottling up inside, or they think that when that comes, it will all work out.

## Do not live today in the future.

For example, we hear couples say, "When we have kids, it'll all work out when you know like our finances are going to come together, and that's just all going to work out." I think acknowledging this is something very important. Some people are like that; they always want to promise something they are going to do in the future when they can do it today. There are certain things we understand you can promise to someone in the future; if you don't have it and you're willing to give it away, then you can promise that.

## Promise in the marriage

That is fair, but why must something you are going to do when you have a better house or promise something you are going to do when you have like a building? When you go to the mall, when you travel out, when you go on vacation, when you have that amount of money, you do not have enough money, those things are not bad, but at the same time, sometimes they are tricky because we do not want to live for the future. We want to make sure we do the best we can today because if we do not do the best we can today, we always will believe in the future. Only answers are going to come together, and that is just all going to work out.

## Being honest

I think, just like acknowledging your own individual fears as far as you like, what if this doesn't happen? How are we going to pivot? How are we going to move forward and go past this? I think you have to be aware of the hopes and dreams of your spouse, like what they're dealing with, and I think that comes from really digging in and being honest. We've talked about being upfront, like saying, "this is what I'm dealing with as far as you know, finances or career." Folks, that's one right here.

## What really changes after one or two, or three days?

I was counseling this young kid that worked for me, and he was in a relationship. It was a horrible relationship. I just sat him down one day, and I said, "the minister told me this one day; he said listen to me when you get married, the only thing that changes the day after you get married is the appearance of your left hand's third finger." People think if they get married, this will solve all their problems. If y'all been arguing the whole time when you get married, you will be arguing the whole time, and nothing will change changes.

## Date the perfect person.

After you get married and don't solve this problem, you don't get it out and open up; if you don't discuss things and you're in a world of you, then you have to understand that when you're dating someone you really know. We often talk about dating the perfect person, they're going to give you all of the good stuff, but when you find red flags, don't let them add up, and it's not going to change. You can't raise a person. We often counsel couples, and we tell them when you date their representative. Come on! my God! You get it, right? You know who you are going to be married to and the man.

I feel like being friends up front and having that person see your authentic self is a plus.

Do you know what it's like to marry the wrong person? There's a scripture that says, "It's better to live on the corner of the rooftop than in the house." You would say, "Don't you rather be outside just catching hell on the roof in the corner and then being there?" That's why I feel like being friends up front with that person and letting them see your authentic self without any obligations or strings attached is the best way. They should know how you look without make-up on or whatever. I remember him when we were friends for seven months. I remember a lot of times we put the other beauty. When talking about beauty, the best is the natural beauty. You can wear makeup, but the natural beauty is what is fair for the other one because when you wear a mask and meet someone, in reality, you don't meet that person because there was a mask until you can take off the mask. Now you're going to see the person you're talking to because in order for you to meet someone, you want to make sure you meet that person. You cannot meet someone in the dark. When it is dark, two people can hear each other but cannot see each other.

## Open your eyes and meet that person

That means if you wear a mask, it means you might never know that person because the beauty that the author in this book like is natural beauty. The way when you wake up from bed, because when you wake up in the bed, you're natural, but after you go to the shower, you wear everything else. Now it becomes like a mask, and nobody can see who you really are until you take off the mask. We want to make sure we talk about reality because sometimes you meet someone, and then you say, wow. This is a beautiful person, and then tomorrow, you meet the same person, and you say, "Now, what's happened to you?" That can happen if the situation changes.

## Healthy Habit

Sometimes someone has a lot of money, allowing them to take care of themselves - eat healthy, and have healthy habits. But if they don't have money certain things can change. You're not going to miss everything because that person was real, but if it was like a mask, you're going to see that everything is different. Therefore, this is what we want to make sure we talk about. Going to underline some extremely specific things you need to do when you date someone or in the marriage.

## Compatibility in choosing your partner

So, you can have a successful marriage; this is what we're talking about today so much emphasis on attraction. Yes, and the truth of the matter is everybody that you are attracted to is not necessarily compatible with you. So you know you might be attracted to them, their looks, but that doesn't mean you can live with them. I'm telling you, man, everybody you are attracted to isn't compatible with. It is not good till it is not permanent. Times aren't done that. Lord, she is fine. Some people have a vision. If we've taken the Bible, we're going to see Joseph was someone that God talked to. Joseph and his dreams and show him so many things, and here's the order.

## God can choose for you

He could explain the dream; if someone else has a dream, he could understand what it is and can tell you the meaning of the dream. So, for now, I remember there was a place they called "the church" where they used to choose for people like the pastor can say or their leader; I'm not going to say pastor, the leader can say, "God, choose that man for that Lady." I used to hear stuff like that. Some days those people do not even love each other, but that can happen. Those with a vision; God can show you certain things, especially if you pray for something, and then you fast for it, and spend time praying about it, believe me, especially when you choose someone in your life. It's something you can do.

## A sign or a Vision

God is going to give you some ideas. Some people even used to ask God for a sign because sometimes they don't ask God to give them a vision about it because they might say, "I'm not a prophet, so God will not tell me certain things." I know there are a lot of people who don't believe in dreams and revelations. That's okay. God said to some people in the bible, "I'm going to give you the first letter." They did ask God for a sign, and He gives you a sign about the person that you need the sign about.

## Love is not a cultural topic but a biblical one

Spirits accept God's instructions and do them. Their homes will be extraordinarily successful. Number one, love is not a cultural topic but a biblical one, that responsibility is the ultimate key. Love is the key that a man uses to transform his wife into a glorious woman without a wrinkle or spot, for the husband is the head of the wife, just as Christ is the head of the church and he is the savior of the body. Husbands! Love your wives, as Christ also loved the church and gave himself for it. So that he might sanctify and cleanse it.

## He that loved his wife loved himself

With the washing of water by the word that he might present it to himself at the glorious church, not having a spot or wrinkle. It should be holy and without blemish. Man, you love your wives as your own bodies. *He that loved his wife loved themselves, for no man ever hated his own flesh. He nourishes it and cherishes it, as the Lord loved the church.* Nevertheless, every one of you loves his wife as himself, and the wife should see that she reveres her husband. Ephesians 5 verses 23 to 33.

Therefore, the transformation of life lies in the hands of the husband. If you really want a glorious wife without a spot or wrinkle, holy and pure, love your wife as your own body. By doing so, you will have created a glorious wife to have a majestic home. Love is the price you pay. This love must be without hypocrisy.

This love sees the good even while assessing a wrong situation. Man, if you want a wife that follows your leadership, you must be a super-duper-loving husband, in all honesty. It is the fastest way to win your life once a man gets to love his wife; as much as Christ loves the church, the devil is closed off from accessing his home.

You must be in love at all times should any unwholesome words go ahead out of your mouth. The first word, "love," is expressed in communication. Without communication, there is no love. This is what we call seasoned communication, Ephesians 5 verse 20. To sanctify her, cleanse her by the washing with water through the word, this man, we expect to cleanse lives by the washing of water by the word, and that implies that every word of your mouth must be seasoned with salt, giving grace to the hero Colossians 4 verse 6 so that you may know how to answer everyone. Love must be behind every observation you make when you correct, instruct or rebuke your wife. It should be love motivating the roots of every speech; you must be in love at all times. Should any unwholesome words go ahead out of your mouth to your wife, raise your children that way. You will present her to your own self as a glorious bride, not having a wrinkle. Likewise, her husband dwells with them according to knowledge, giving honor to the wife as the weaker vessel and being an heir of life's grace so that your prayers are not handed. Peter chapter 3, verse 7. Husbands are obligated to honor their wives, as it is the grace of life. This obviously removes actions like beating, humiliating, or maltreating the woman.

## It is the man's responsibility to be involved in his wife's affairs

God expects you to deal with your wife according to the knowledge of the truth. He will help you such that. If your wife has a terrible character, you can change her through the knowledge of the truth. It is the man's responsibility to be involved in his wife's affairs. Some husbands clearly see something wrong in the home and yet pretend that all is well. God will take control, they say, but that is not right. God has given man a leadership position in the home. Have you ever seen a driver taking his hands off the steering wheel and saying, "God, take control; I am tired."

## Man, God has given you control as the head of the home

An accident is inevitable. God has given you control as the head of the home. Be a smart driver; otherwise, that family is heading for an accident. For instance, if you notice your wife is downcast, you should ask her. You must not open your home to malice or discord. It can prevail over them all by knowledge. Giving is a practical expression of love for God. He so loves the world that He sends Jesus to take away everyone's sin, and whosoever believeth in him should not perish but have everlasting life. John three verse 16. One of the ways a husband should express his love for his wife is by giving gifts to his wife willingly and joyfully. The quantity is not the issue here. We are all at diverse levels of life.

## Repeat the love habit through the ages

The husband must accept his responsibility by happily giving his wife gifts. That is what counts. Some men shy away from responsibilities and do not give their wives anything. This is done under the guidance of the modern world where the wives are working. This does not change the fact that man must look to give as the scripture says. But if a man supplies not for his own and especially for those in his own house, he has denied the faith and is worse than an infidel. First, Timothy chapter 5, verse 8. It is the man's responsibility to support the home. Even if she makes an income or not. When a man inherently stops looking after his household, it has a spiritual significance in his life.

## You must be concerned about your wife and your children's wellbeing

Man's life becomes worse than that of an unbeliever. God says that he has denied the faith and will suffer the same fate as unbelievers. You must be concerned about your wife and your children's wellbeing.

## Violation of the covenant obligations

Some husbands leave their homes without any concern. The family members not having eaten or not behaving is a significant violation of the covenant obligations. No man has a right to wear new clothes if his family is going out in rags.

# Financial obligations

He should set aside some resources from whatever he earned to take care of the personal needs of his household. A good man leaves an inheritance to his children. The sin is also laid up for the righteous, proverbs 13 verse 22. You should have a monthly percentage for everyone in the household. Even the children should have their own personal accounts. He must share the word of God, not from his wife's income. He must set up a percentage of his earnings for her; remember that if we want to give the advice needed to have a better life in this society today, because when we consider the ancient war, the ancient people, the world, we are living today the technology is well advanced.

# Marriage in ancient times and marriage today

“The advancement of technology.” That means we have a lot we can discuss because we must make sure we talk about reality because we are living in 2023. Today is January 3rd, 2023, which means we cannot have any idea about someone who lived 50 years ago. Some advice would be best for us but do not forget that we live in January 3rd, 2023, which means we cannot compare certain things that happened 100 years ago. We can compare certain things in life, like a preacher. As Stanley said last Sunday, “the 1st Sunday of the year that we need to forget about the past, we need to forget about the past when I say forget about the past.” Women, we need to remember today; we want to make sure we have the focus on what we are doing and what we are going to do tomorrow. That’s because yesterday is a testimony. This is what I always say.

## A plan is necessary

Yesterday is a testimony, today is a gift, and tomorrow will be the future. The future is coming, prepare for it. Yesterday is the result of the day before yesterday, and today is the result of yesterday. That means the result of today is going to be tomorrow. I want to make sure I understand it. I will make sure I do something because the day has 24 hours. I want to make sure I use my 24 hours to create something on my own, with my own thinking, with my own idea, because building something from scratch means you have an idea about it.

## You have the idea, and you know how to develop it

We are not going to build anything. If you do not know what you are doing, it is not going to make sense. For anything that you do, you must make sure you know it very well and work on it every day, so you can be successful. Do not forget we are discussing marriage, a particularly important matter for us. We are going to give you some ideas about the law because when we talk, we want to make sure we tell you about God because God is the one that instituted the marriage.

## Today's Marriage

At the same time, we want to make sure we tell you about the reality of today. How to live a healthy, happy life in the modern days. We want to make sure we talk about that in this book, so this book is going to be good for those who are getting married or those who are about to get married; so if someone needs an idea of how to live a better life in marriage today, this book is for you.

This book is for you because you are going to find in this book verses from the Bible, all the verses and all the words that you need to know to have a successful marriage, not how much that matters but accepting your responsibility and doing it joyfully. Where you are now is a good place to start. You should have access to everything you own.

## Concern about her well-being

In fact, all that is yours is hers. You must love her with all your being. Everything that concerns her well-being must also be a concern for you. We want to make sure we talk about marriage. Some people think talking about marriage possession is like everything the man has because, in my understanding and the Haitian view, when two people are married, they don't have a contract. What they have is that they are just getting married. They do not have a contract that means whatever the lady owns is for the man, and whatever the man owns is for the lady. That means if those people are going to be separated, it is going to be equal. For both, that means we are not going to talk about separation because we want to make sure we are talking about marriage

There are different types of marriages.

We do not see anything about separation. Everything is good but is not good for others, especially about possession, because the idea might be good because, in the United States, where we are citizens, there are different types of marriages. Not all people are in a marriage, or all people that are married are living in a marriage. No, it is different. Some people even have an end date for the marriage. That's why we want to ensure we tell you according to the Bible. We tell you about the Bible because not everything you are going to hear about the word marriage is what I want to tell you today because I tell you what God said about marriage and how we can live it. Today in society. The importance of this book is Fifty, fifty.

In marriage, they have their own contracts. They say what they need in their marriage. We, as Christians, need to get married according to the word of God. This is what we want to talk about. Other things might not be that important. Talking about the position, what the man has is for the lady, and what the lady has is for the man. We're not most likely talking about possession, but we want to make sure we talk about the main importance of marriage and how people can build a marriage that will be a family in the future, for years and for life

## God expects you to nourish her

This is what we want to talk about. Give you the heart to love your family. You must love your wife and her deeds, and not only in words, if you may ask because God expects you to nourish her as you would nourish yourself. We pray that God will strengthen you.

## When people have issues, they cannot live healthily

Trying to learn how to submit to my husband was one of the hardest things for me; in anything, it didn't matter to me if it was right or wrong or indifferent I just didn't want to be bossed around. I was mistreated by a man in my childhood, my father sexually abused me, and he was very mean, manipulative, and controlling. I made a covenant with myself that when I get out of here, nobody is ever going to tell me what to do again, and I promised myself that for years and let me tell you when I finally saw that was not the will of God there were some things in this woman's flesh that had to be broken. This is called when people have issues; some people cannot live healthily in the marriage. It's because they had some issues in the past before they got married. They have some reality in their lives that prevent them from having a good marriage, and that is the reason why we want to make sure we talk about the word of God and what the Bible says about it.

## When people have issues, they cannot live healthily

Trying to learn how to submit to my husband was one of the hardest things for me; in anything, it didn't matter to me if it was right or wrong or indifferent I just didn't want to be bossed around. I was mistreated by a man in my childhood, my father sexually abused me, and he was very mean, manipulative, and controlling. I made a covenant with myself that when I get out of here, nobody is ever going to tell me what to do again, and I promised myself that for years and let me tell you when I finally saw that was not the will of God there were some things in this woman's flesh that had to be broken. This is called when people have issues; some people cannot live healthily in the marriage. It's because they had some issues in the past before they got married. They have some reality in their lives that prevent them from having a good marriage, and that is the reason why we want to make sure we talk about the word of God and what the Bible says about it.

## Disagreement in marriage

There was a testimony by a lady; she said she would forget about when they talked about the problem. As something happened, they said they wanted to reconcile. And she said she had forgotten about it. The next time they talk about something, she will not reveal or repeat what happened in the past. She leaves it in the past and keeps going, which means some people cannot live a good marriage. It is because they already have something that they are not going to forgive, it is not the same person, but it is a reality they have that does not work.

We want to make sure we talk about certain things that for those that are married, maybe they live in that situation today, maybe they in this situation are the problem. However, they don't even realize they are the problem because that's their mindset. It is something in the mind that prevents them from knowing that they are wrong, but they want to make sure they bring it to other people or try not to understand reality. They will try to create certain things that do not even exist for the other person. This is what we wanted to talk about. Now, we have that other testimony that gave us a real-life testimony about this disobedient lady. She said about how she talked, and she is not going to have any respect for him.

## Communication problems

If I say that the wife doesn't have any regard for the husband, how do you think this marriage will be OK if they cannot have the conversation the way they should have it, according to the marriage rules, as I mentioned earlier. I can remember hurting so badly over simple little things that Dave would ask me to do or not to do, and I would just go wild, you know. The more rebellion you have in your flesh, the wilder you are going to act. I mean, I can remember having a three-day fit over a bathroom towel. I had to call God on my life. I was already teaching home Bible study, and God had called me to preach the gospel to the world. I had a seed of it in my spirit, but you know what was in me could not get out unless the flesh was broken. I had an embryo of greatness in me, but I was never going to see it manifested if I was going to throw a three-day fit over a bathroom towel. Is anybody home today? I did not want my husband. He was an engineer before entering the ministry, and he just watched everything, including me.

## How a wife perceives the husband

I mean, he thinks that I would not even think of, and really there are good things or things that will keep me safe, but I don’t like all of that. You’ll tell me, “oh! Don’t get out of the bathtub!” like that’s a real-life story about marriage, the lady speaking and letting you know about her behavior in the marriage, so that means when you have lived that way. You will understand as a lady how you’re going to reach your own marriage and as a man how you are going to deal with something like that. For example, when you’re not home, I take a bath, and you know, it's hard; he just has that protective thing in him that a man should have over his wife.

## Obedience in the relationship.

But because of what I had in me, I didn't take that as loving me. I took it as him trying to tell me what to do. I had one of those mornings, and this was many years ago, where I just said, "God, I just really want to have my coffee this morning, just be left alone," but no, you better count on it. So I started, I got in the shower, and threw my towel on the toilet seat. The toilet was over there, the shower was over here, and David did not put up a towel rack yet, which I had been asking him to do like forever. Therefore, I couldn't hang the towel on the shower door because there was no rack on the door, so I put it on the toilet seat. I got in the shower, got out, stepped on the floor dripping, and got my towel.

When these types of behavior happen in marriage, it is a big red flag for the marriage.

Even hear what he said because the attitude that is in us will always come out. These are unruly behaviors in marriage and a big red flag for the marriage, and it depends on how the men will handle the situation. Like that only the Bible a man equation a man with a Bible can handle the situation. This is how I understand it, and we know we're going to know the outcome of that situation because there are so many ladies like that, and there are some difficult medals, so we want to make sure we understand the problem to form some people that tell exactly the way.

# Who's fault is it?

They behave in a mouth that they feel that it is unfair, so other people can understand that and say, "No, I'm not going to behave like that because it is unfair."

I mean and say, which was my automatic response, "Well, what is wrong with me putting my towel there."

"Well, you're dripping water on the floor."

"I said, 'Well, it is the bathroom, and not only that if you would have put the towel rack on the door like I've asked you to, a million times, then there wouldn't be a problem!" They say right away when we're rebellious, it's not our fault, and don't try to tell us. It is because it's your fault. Well, I just got mad, and he went on about his business. I was moaning to God after crying out that I couldn't even shower peacefully. I just wanted to have one cup of coffee and just be left alone.

Many people pray for their ministries and finances to grow, and there's no end to it. You got to tell me what to do; well, God, I just don't think I can stand this anymore. Now, keep it in mind, I had a call on my life to reach the world and little ministry, and I can tell you that if I were to stay in that condition, I would still have a little ministry. So many people are praying for their ministries to grow and their finances to grow. God has asked you to do something that involves you dying to self and your flesh being crucified, and you haven't gotten around to doing what God has said yet.

Come on now, we're preaching good tonight, and I remember one morning when I was praying for my ministry to grow. Man, I had been to the intercessory prayer seminar. I had been to the casting out devils seminar, I had been to the spiritual warfare seminar, and I was after it. I rebuke you, Satan, in the name of Jesus.

## God communicates to us

I am a child of the highest God. I command this ministry to grow. You have no authority over me, saying right now in Jesus's name. James and I heard the spirit of God say to me, just as calmly as I am speaking to you right now, He said, "Joyce, I have told you what you need to do concerning your husband, and if you do not do it, then there is no other thing God can talk to us for those who are Christian who is following the principle of God, the Bible the, word of God that those that

That is a real-life testimony, and we wanted to have that in this book to help people get the marriage they deserve from God.

We really take time to read the Bible submissive to God talked to them, especially about how they live what they choose when we already talk about it, and this is what we get from that stimy that is a real-life testimony, and we wanted to have this and in this book to help people getting the marriage they deserve from God because marriage is a very good thing. It's a great institution. It's one institution where I can do any kind of growth. Your ministry silence. I mean, I wanted to talk about it and negotiate to see if we could come up with a less painful plan but let me tell you something. God's finished it. Here comes the pruning shears, and all you're left with is.

## Marriage is for everyone who believes according to the will of God

Already man has a lot of responsibility in marriage today, and the Bible tells us what to do. Some people create some ideas about man's responsibility, but I will not say. It is a good thing. I am not going to say. It is not good when they bring everything over the men like the man handles everything. I am not going to say no to this. Still, I want to ensure I talk about what the Bible says about marriage because society sometimes changes everything.

They tell you something, and then you think it's the best thing when it's something they cannot do. It might be a good thing for some, but it might not be good for others. All situations are not the same, OK, because we want to discuss several types of marriage. Those that don't have a lot of money and those that have millions of dollars because we want to make sure we're talking about something that is fair for everyone, not for those that have the opportunity to do it because marriage is for everyone. No, it's not for one person. Marriage is for everyone, and marriage is not when you have money.

## Wrong motives in marriage

I'm your wife; when you do not, I am not, or when you have the job, I am your husband; if you lose your job, I am not. If you went to university, you keep your university degree, I am going to be your husband if you lose it, or if you do not do that anymore, I am not your husband anymore. We want to ensure that my wage is not like that because some people add certain things to a marriage that are not really a marriage. A university degree is a good thing for marriage; it adds something to it. But this is not marriage. A decent job makes the marriage life a healthy and happy life, but this is not the job that is the marriage, but it is suitable for the marriage. It is going to make marriage better.

## Marriage and Money

Some people have everything they need, but they keep having problems in their marriage. That means this is not the problem. Sometimes it is like what Jesus just said. She didn't. She could not handle the conversation with her husband. Those are the things we want to talk about in this book because some people with a mindset about marriage. Today some men don't want to get married because they don't have enough money. They don't have the job they need to get married, but we're going to talk about that too because we have the experience to tell you, for those that don't have enough that is required to get married, and for those that have enough money.

## You are the house born; that is why they call you a father

Looking at this word the other day, I realized that a man's power in the family is the key to the family. As a matter of fact, the word "husband" is two words put together. The first is the word "house," born one of the parents in the house together. If you are the husband, your job is like glue; you are supposed to glue the whole family together. You are responsible for gluing the family together. You are the house born. That's why they call you a father. The word father is the people's word "ABBA." It means "source" and "sustainer." Not just the source, you got to sustain with your source, that's my baby good are you paying for the school of that baby, are you feeding that child, who by the way did you know that women are your baby too, God did not take women from the soil.

## It is natural for the man to call his wife "baby."

He went inside the male and pulled out her feet for the male. That's what I like about God. No other words. The male came out, but he built the male to make him a female, so a real female is a female because she has a wound to carry the fetus. You are a female if you get a fetus capacity, so you could break your wrist where your earring you aren't got no woman. Your job is to sustain your baby; the woman came out of man, not man. Crap, that means the female in your life is your baby; that's why it's natural for a man to call his wife "baby." It's in your genes. She's your baby. That means you must feed her, clothe her, protect he, counsel her, provide for her, everything, but right, she's a young baby. No, I didn't want sex; that's your problem,

## The family is like a business corporation

The house should be bonded together by the house born. The family is like a business corporation; the father is the president, the wife's the vice president, the children are the board members, and the neighbors are clients. Now, look at this voice carefully. You are the president, which means you preside. You don't own or control. You preside over the house, who's your wife, the vice president.

The mission is to don't act without getting advice from your wife as well. Oh, I'm in trouble now. See, your children are on the board, which means you inform them of what you're doing and why you're doing it. You're going to run the house together. It has to be a corporate effort management. The home is the greatest test of a man's leadership. What did I say? I can't hear you say it again. Management of the home is the greatest test of a man's leadership; that's why the apostle Paul says, "look, if you want to come into God's house and sit on this pulpit," he says, "first you must manage your own whole." Well, there are some men who want to build a house with God, but they can't build their own house. They're men who come to other people's kids for losing their own kids.

## Man must be the boss of the home

Some men spend more time with other women than with their wives, and they call it counseling. You all do not get quiet because I am going to walk right down there. Talk to somebody who needs to make an appointment to see there is your wife, one of them; she wants to see you here and talk to her for months. You are the manager of that home.

## How is the marriage going to be successful?

Ephesians explains the responsibility of a wife. In Ephesians 5, we want to stick to the Bible and make sure we explain the marriage responsibility either for the man or the lady. This is what we want to do today, and we want to make sure everyone, either a man or a woman, knows their responsibility. As christian, they're going to say, "Yes, I'm going to do as the Bible says," and now you're going to have a successful marriage. If you don't do that, that might be why your wife is really leaving you, because you have constant fighting and bickering about the marriage foundation.

If you want to know how to be a good wife to your husband, you've come to the right place. Now I won't be able to give you the whole deal. For that, you could use either one of my books, "Breaking the cycle" or "Lessons for a happy marriage," but I'm going to give you a warning. If you're doing this now because your husband is leaving you or because he's starting to go on dating sites, it's too late for that basic education. Now you need to take the course for women that we offer, which will help you turn the whole thing around because it's gone too far, but hopefully, that's not where you're at. Hopefully, you're just realizing, you know, I could be a better wife and knock his socks off.

## Each partner is there to make the other happy

You know what happens are we get married in order to be happy, and then the happiness fades because no one tells us that. We don't do anything to make each other happy because that's the whole deal. When you're in a marriage, you are not there to make yourself happy. You're there to make your spouse happy. Doesn't that make sense? They're there to make you happy, but you can't hold them to that. Here's the cosmic secret to it all, the more love you give, the more love you feel it's true. It's a very deep spiritual reality.

## Stop blaming the other partner

It is as strong as gravity, but no one told you that, so when you got married. You started having expectations of how he would treat you rather than having of yourself and how you would treat him. I've seen all this cause I was a divorce mediator before. People would come in and see me and oh, he did this, she did that, blah blah blah. It was all blame. They had hated each other by the time they came to see me and it was made worse because they were sent to me by a therapist. God bless those who failed them. They went to a therapist to heal their marriage and they failed, which is usual. People don't know that but it's the truth and so I had one couple come in and I said, OK, why are you getting a divorce, and they both started crying.

## Negotiation can save your marriage

"We don't want. We don't know what else to do," they said. I said OK. Let me try and figure it out. I know a few things about communication; at that time, I thought everything was communication. If you learn how to communicate if you learn how to negotiate, it tells you a little bit about my practice, which was divorce mediation. I left the office that day, and they were very excited. "We can save our marriage!" It worked there. I was like, "oh my God! What did I get myself into? What am I going to do."

## The purpose you are getting married

I couldn't ask the therapist. I asked a couple of them what I should do, and they went, "Well, you know, find out about their childhood."

Then I'm like, "No, I'm not a therapist. I don't care about their childhood."

"We'll find out about influences from in-laws, influences from work." I'm going, "No, that doesn't sound right to me. It's not right."

You go through troubles in life. Who doesn't? But when you're married, you're supposed to go through them together, giving each other strength and support. So, I thought, OK. I got to start someplace. Let me start with a question, "Why did you get married?" And it went, "Oh my God! I didn't know the answer then, and for a couple of weeks, I worked on it and started asking my friends. I started asking people I didn't know.

I would be in the Starbucks line. I go, "I got a question for you." No one had a good answer, and everyone had a good answer, like, "oh, I married my soulmate because...."

## Why did you want to get married?

They are blah blah, oh you know, I just wanted to be with someone who, I would not be alone, I wanted to have children, you know, good answers, but they were not universal to me. It did not sound like this was the ultimate took me a while to realize, so what is the answer to the question, "Did you get married cause you want to be happier?" Good. Well, those things will make you happy when, not universally, not everyone wants a child. Some people want to spend time by themselves in the woods or knitting or whatever, and I thought about what universally makes you happy, love that.

## Love and its barriers

I started probing this question, and I realized some very deep realities. Here's one which will blow your mind. If you follow Jesus or Moses or Mohammed, the all-time great prophet from God that came to you at this very moment and gave you love. You would not allow it in because you have these protective barriers, and I thought that's true. Isn't it? Think about it. I thought, "So how does this work?" and I realized how it works is that you got to give love. I'll tell you how I discovered this. I discovered this because I have kids, and the time I like the best is when I would watch them sleep, and my heart would just open up, and I recalled that my heart just opened up.

## The love you give allows God's love to flow at greater levels

They weren't saying daddy, and I love you. You're the greatest; oh my God, your hair is so beautiful. I wasn't kidding you. I felt more love in those moments than at any other time. This is pretty cool, and I realize it's not the love you give that will bring love back. That's not how it works. That's what people think, but that's not how it works. The love you give allows God's love because God is the ultimate one. God's love flows through you at a greater and greater level based on using your free will, and it fills you with love. I now had a premise to go back to my first couple, and I said, "OK, here's the deal. What are the things that create love, what are loving behaviors, what are things that are not loving behaviors?" and laid it all out anyway. They did it with me. We did it together not so hard, then it got a little more complicated, but I'm not going to get into that now. Look, in your case, you could probably do it if your marriage is not nosediving and if it's not speeding toward divorce. If you don't see divorce on the horizon, and you're not fooling yourself about it, I lay it all out of it. I hold nothing back.

## What is the secret to a healthy and happy marriage?

And life has secrets because when you see something, sometimes you like a mystery. For you, most likely, people think there's a secret behind this. But for marriage, is there any secret for marriage?

We're going to look at marriage today to see if there is any secret you need to know to have a successful marriage. A lot of people have absolutely no framework because we live in an era of the collapse of marriage. In our society, the complete sort of breakdown of the family union unit that you were describing a moment ago, doctor Philippe and so Andrea asked what is the secret to a healthy and happy marriage. I think that's actually a very well-composed question for a healthy and happy marriage.

## The answer for a happy marriage.

Drew, I got 42 years with my wife, and she may be here tonight. If he hasn't gotten up and gone home, you know, I used to answer that it was simple politeness, treating each other with kindness, but then I realized what I was really saying is that it's gratitude. It is gratitude for the invisible things your spouse does for you every single day by simply existing and including her and him in your own achievements. My wife is as much part of my ego as I am, her pain is my pain, and her joy is my joy. I hope she feels that way about me, I think that takes time to establish, and kindness and gratitude are the way to take that time until you're so much one entity that you just feel with each other and care so much for each other that you're there for one another when you need, we can go around this way because I don't want to go after Jeff Peterson. OK, good, I'll allow it. I think that's actually, to be honest.

## A healthy marriage is to root out the spirit of competition

I was going to say gratitude, and I actually have nothing to say now. I think a big key to a healthy marriage is to root out the spirit of competition or at least channel it in a healthy way because a lot of times, especially when you bring kids into the mix, you get into this competitive thing where it's like well I did this around the house. I was up with the kid in the middle of the night for X amount of hours. You're not doing this, and you've got the scorecard you're keeping score all the time, and that's why I think it's so toxic these days when you hear from people that will marriage is supposed to be 50:50 in order to be 50 feet 50 equal partners, and that's exactly the wrong approach because then you're always measuring well I'm at 49 right now. You're at 51. You both just give yourselves 100%, and don't worry about competition. You channel the competition through board games in your marriage. You take board games very seriously. My wife and I have just gone to bed angry at each other because of board games before; like the Bible says today, that's okay as long as it's for board games. We'll ban board games in my house with my husband.

## Until you have children

I decided to play scrabble, and we realized he had English spelling of words, so obviously, "honor" is not spelled with "EU." We're in America. This is America. I have to say that for the record, but I'm going to kind of say my last answer again and restate the symbiotic nature of masculinity and femininity. I'm not trying to be my husband; he's not trying to be me, and especially when you have children, you realize how children really grow when they have both. The things my husband is concerned about when it comes to our child care things that I don't even think twice about what he needs that maternity and that paternity and

## Think twice, plan your marriage

It's just beautiful to see how right the Bible is on absolutely everything. Attested to it is a statement actually by the greatest Jewish common commentator theater Dennis Prager. I thank you, I would take it slightly differently. What to avoid rather than what to do, and there were two things that I think people need to avoid. One is this; "taking the other for granted." I think people should rest their life when they try to win that person to be a spouse; you look at how much, and then within a year or ten years or 2023 years, it all goes to hell. I stopped trying to win this person. My favorite English verb is "earn." It's one of the only languages in the world that has the word in all Latin languages, which are you

## Doctor Philippe's answer

I say, win an income in America, any English who say, "I earn the other one is my happiness," that you are not allowed to inflict your bad mood on others any more than you can inflict your bad mood on other issues. Your upper apple gave it is to wash away you're bad blue just as you wash away, you're bad mood someone named him to ask him what is the name and I'm going to answer to the question by going and going after doctor Philippe. Well, I actually don't think it's a good question, and I'll tell you what I mean. I think being happy is a pretty low goal. First of all, well, there are going to be lots of types of times in terms of New York married rich, where you are seriously not happy, and sometimes that's going to be because you're having conflict with your partner, but sometimes it's going to be because all broke loose and surround you and then if you judge the success of your marriage on you have your happiness like and the same thing happening if there's a future success in life on the basis of yourself you're happy what do you have with win it's not, but such suffering during that's, it's going to be plenty of tea of life.

## The mood

I would just like to make serving all this. No, it is not what you expect. This is a whole dialog that would be inconceivable at any left-wing place, and then the reason is that we really hate it. Reality is none of this discussion, especially the last comment. No, I could prove it. This will take just literally under. If you want your husband to be a good man, and if you respect him, if he treats you beautifully, then don't only allow your mood to determine whether you sleep with him.

That was the thesis of it, of course, there are times when obviously that will determine but do not pull away, ways just this mood could not determine open almost anything think good that we do I don't determine whether and the right I after listening saying I just want to give one another because after to think all.

## Complaining husband

Particular marriage, and that is the system. Stop pitching bing now. The same advice could go to women, but there is no point in that. I think I know you ladies, and you open the floodgates, so I'm just jumping. I think we've long lost the sentence of self-stoicism in men. They complain completely in marriages just, and so now, because we encourage management, and we don't like to be very open about it, you remove your emotions, and what ends up happening is that you like dumb Bombay.

Talk about important things, do not waste your time and energy on things that are not important.

The importance of the sentence is that we feel real with an enlarged. Live if it's not my matter, why should we have a word for it? Sometimes we don't have anything for something, thinking it just because it's good this is not matter. It's not essential if it's Doctor Philippe. Put intent. We should consider redirection, and we should value and use something that is important that you want to talk about. Why wait?

Today my mother is the mother who far as who child by refusing photoprotection things hemmer her so instead of being strengthened by counter winter with her with the terrible world, they're No suggested we can be too much protection and then they're let out into the world you're not living in then. That's the story of Sleeping Beauty, and that's what the cooking and queen do. They apologized to Melissa when she first showed up. They have a bunch of halves and wouldn't have excuses like "why this," "why that," "why they didn't invite her," or "we forgot." God, it's like I don't know. Thank you so much, and you know you don't forget something like that. She is going to make sense of that point; it's right.

## A little talk about baby or considerations

The whole horror of life is that you don't forget or get a doubt that when you have a child, that's for sure. You might wish that it would stay with that baby, but you do not forget about it. The question is, just do you invite headed to the party? Then the answer is, "it bloody well depends on how well 11 columns are conscious. Tell the beat, and if you want your child conscious, then you have the added maybe they won't leave home, so you can take advantage of them. Take them for the rest of your servers your sad life instead of going on off to give something to do for yourself well, and then, of course, you can take revenge on them if they tell who has it. Have anyway what would you call important to this towards Kurt courage that you used yourself 12, 30, or 30 years ago and to go and stamp out as you see it developing in your child? That's another thing to be quite pleasant.

You know that people who live together before marriage are more likely to get divorced.

Two things come off of that; one is that people are waiting around to find Mr. or Mrs. Right. It's like, here's something to think about. To put yourself on your feet right. If you went to a party and you found Mr. Right, and he looked at you and didn't run away screaming, that would indicate that he wasn't Mr. Wright at all. It's like the old Nietzsche joke: "If someone loves you, they should immediately disenchant you." With them right, it's the Woody Allen joke. I never belonged to a club that would take me as a member, so that's interesting. That's a very interesting thing to think about, and so you're going to shackle yourself to someone who's just as imperfect as you are, and then the issue is you might be in a situation where you can actually negotiate because you might think well there's something going about me which is not right.

## Dilemma

And so we can either straighten this out, or we can suffer through it for the next five decades. People are of the sort that without that degree of seriousness, those problems will not be solved. You'll leave things unnamed because there's always an out. It's like it's the same thing when you're living together with someone. You know that people who live together before they're married are more likely to get divorced, not less likely, and the reason for that is what exactly are you saying to one another when you live with each other? Just think about it. Well, for now, you're better than anything else I can trick, but I'd like to reserve the right to trade you in conveniently if someone better happens to stumble into me just had such a massive,

That is one way of thinking about it. That is the most fundamental conception of humankind; something like that is the unknown and then the bifurcation of that into the two fundamental cognitive elements of human perception.

That's exactly like, "I know you're not going to commit to me; that means you don't value me or our relationship above everything else, but as long as I get to escape, if I need to, then I'm willing to put up with that." It's like that's a hell of a thing. I mean, you might think how stupid it is to shackle yourself to someone. It's stupid, man, there's no doubt about that, but compared to the alternatives, it's pretty good because, without that shackling, there are things you will never ever learn because you'll avoid them. You can always leave, and if you can leave, then you don't have to tell each other the truth. It's as simple as that because you can just leave, and then you don't have anyone you can tell the truth, so there are some representations of the idea of the original. It's not that this isn't all. Adam, this is an old Chinese symbol. I think it's foxie. Now although I think I have the parts of pronunciation wrong, but it's really cool. See, it's the snakes down here. They're kind of like a DNA symbol which I find very interesting. So that's the original cosmic serpent that's sort of the potential out of which that emerges. Then that's the differentiation of that into male and female. So that's like the predatory unknown that's one way of thinking about it.

# The most fundamental conception of humankind

The most fundamental conception of mankind, something like that, is probably unknown, and then the bifurcation of that into the two fundamental cognitive elements of human perception, “masculine” and “female.” You see the same thing here. This is Chinese, and this is Egyptian, also extraordinarily old. It’s the great serpent that underlies everything now defecate pictures of how can I know the person and how can I make a decision. Last one, but it’s hot. Listen, some of you are too dramatic when you want to marry someone, and then this is the Qatar of God.,

# Some advice about breaking the marriage engagement

He is perfect, and then when he says, I want to break the engagement. How? I don’t understand the philosophy of Qatar because the engagement broke marriage is an informed decision. Families come together, and you do the best you can to understand. If this is a good decision for you and it’s like any other decision, my dear daughter, my dear son, my younger brother, my younger sister. This is like any other decision. Nobody writes a question, “Is buying God is eating a chicken sandwich this afternoon for lunch the cadre of God?” No, all the other decisions are your responsibility. Marriage, God, where did you get this idea from? Make an informed decision, learn about the person you are trying to marry, understand if you have a personality that will work with each other, and even after all the exploration and conversation, sometimes you know what happens.

You cannot escape drama. Yes, sometimes drama happens. Anyway, it ends up being an interesting life. Our Seattle, the 11, entered ended up with a firm for a husband. Do not raise your hand; your husband's not fit. Calm down; sometimes people change, and sometimes the person you married later they are different from what they used to be the way.

## Those are details not from the Bible

They have changed. Maybe life has changed you, and maybe experiences changed you. Don't blame that on the counter of God. That's not the culture of God. That's life. It happens. Our dream is beautiful; it's absolutely beautiful. It gave us a way to understand the marriage relationship. The advice I will give you about marriage, one thing I will tell you about marriage that people don't pay attention to is, "I want to marry her because I love her, man because I want to marry him for Deen. You're not marrying a beard; you're marrying a human. It's a person. You could be a religious person, pray five times, and you could still hate their cuts. Just because someone is practicing their Deen does not make them a good person.

## What takes away the peace? If love is there, peace is not there (Not the Biblical)

In every other way, there are plenty of people that have an anger problem. They go to hedge every year, but they still have anger problems. So what I'm trying to mention, the one thing about marriage that is on top number one, everything else is later, is this; He said he gave, he made you into his spouse for the purpose that you could find peace for what purpose. See it. You could find peace and then two and three, vagina Benaka that's two and three number one is peace. Now, what does that mean? That means when you love someone, but they sometimes love you, you can love someone without respecting them. You can love someone without being honest with them. You can love someone without caring for them. Properly you can love someone but hate their family, and all of these things, what they do, they take away the peace. So even if love is there, peace is not there.

## Helpful details but not from the Bible

When peace is not there, the purpose of the marriage is gone. The purpose is not the love that comes from love; the purpose is not to care Rahman that comes from God. Your purpose is to find peace, so when you're looking for a spouse, you should ask yourself, "What is it that makes me peaceful? What is it that gives me calm?" My wife, my husband. This should be my calm when I talk to them. My stress goes down, my anxiety goes down, and my anger disappears because of all the storms in my life; my spouse gets rid of them. That's the kind of person I want to marry. Now if you're talking to someone and already there's drama, there's already a temper problem, there's already attitude, there's already difficulty in communication, and you're ignoring it because you love him too much, then you're not going to have peace later. You're just simply not going to have it. This is actually the primary objective, and young men and women, when you get married, the most important conversation is going to be what gives you peace.

## Helpful details but not from the Bible

Tell me, what gives you peace? How can I give you that peace, and what gives you peace? How can I give you that peace? Lita school Leha, so you could give each other a piece you give each other Sakina. That's it. What most people suffer in marriages is drama. No peace, no peace, young man! University students, stay out of trouble. Stay in good company, and stay purposeful. Young women, when you're learning in a university or college, stop having anxiety. "Who's going to marry me? When am I going to get married? When is the Cadillac going to come?" Stop! Just do your homework. Stop. The last thing is when you live a purposeful life, when you accomplish a purpose, and you live that way, then good people of purpose will come into your life. You won't have to look for that spouse; that spouse will look for you. You have to just become purposeful, and you can do it. You're smart; you're creative. God has given you an opportunity. You're Christians. You are perfect.

## Conciseness

It will get more encouraging and confident for you, believe it or not. When you study the subject of marriage throughout history, it's sketchy. Furthermore, when you study the subject of marriage in the Bible, it's not quite as vivid as we probably like it to be. So, how do we piece this whole thing together? Well, this is what we do know definitively. In Genesis, right away, the first words recorded by a man were a covenant ceremony, which is why we use similar words of an atom for our marriage ceremonies. "Today, this is bone of my flesh, and it shall become one till death do us part."

This was all the language that was buried inside Adam's Hebrew vow to eat. Furthermore, as we progress, we see that it was an assumed thing based on Adam and Eve that a man shall leave his father and mother and cleave to his wife. So right away, we're told that there is that union. There is that relationship, and then as you progress all the way through the Old Testament. You see, husband and wife are clearly depicted. Now, what you don't see is how that happened. We've got to be careful because we do have some historical narratives telling us in some cultures, at sometimes, some details. How about the picking of wives, selecting of wives? How about Rachel and Leah? Is that the way we're supposed to do it? Work for seven years, and you get what you go for. Oh no! that was like a deal that was cultural, maybe.

## What makes a marriage a marriage?

It just seemed to happen, so it's a historical narrative. Nevertheless, what did we see, though? We saw that there was a wedding ceremony of some sort, and we also saw that there was consummation. Now, please note some folks take the consummation as the actual. That's when the wedding is actually sealed. When that act takes place, do we see what's definitively described in the Bible? I don't think we do. We see it displayed, but we don't see it as "what makes a marriage a marriage."

Now, let's fast forward to the New Testament. What do we see there? The betrothal of Mary and Joseph, and we do know from history. Now it does get a little bit clearer in the 1st-century Jewish culture what that marriage looked like. How it came about? By way of oodles of biblical illustrations regarding the second coming of Jesus Christ, nevertheless.

## Marriage Commitment

If you were in a biblical covenant in God's eyes, another theme throughout the old instrument, is the covenant relationship.

We see a betrothal, and we see a ceremony. We see a promise of commitment; do we see the vows? No, we don't. Who was the mouse in the government of Rome? Was it a rabbi? Was it the family? How did that happen? I don't. We don't know. Really, Paul talks about marriage a lot in first Corinthians. He describes that there is a ceremony that must have happened that brought a man and woman together, and it's valid in the eyes of God. Even though they didn't cut if you were a biblical covenant in God's eyes, another theme throughout the old instrument, that is in covenant relationship.

We know that it's an actual marriage because Paul says you can't get divorced. You were married as a Pagan to a Pagan. You can't get divorced. Now that you're a Christian because it's valid, how did that ceremony go down? If physicians, we read about what that marriage is, a picture of the gospel, and we do see the relationship. It's defined what the roles are. What it was always intended to put, intended to point toward, but how did somebody get into that relationship? Oh no, so now here's what we're left with. We're left with some definitive, and we're left with some sketchy here's the sketchy part.

## God makes it clear it is a real covenant

We don't know in every custom, in every chapter of the Bible where marriage is discussed, how they got into that relationship. Here's the overwhelming message of the Bible. There is a relationship, and there must be something formal to it. What would I do in harmonizing the two if God didn't make it clear? How could you get into it? There's some room for fudging on this, and that's throughout generations and societies and cultures. Nevertheless, we do see definitively there is some sort of covenant-making ceremony that must take place in order for God to see a man and a woman as being of 1 flesh.

There's a contract that is cut. It's oral, it's typically codified, and we used to do it in front of our bibles. Now, we have a marriage ceremony and a state license from the state. Nevertheless, there is something contractual about it; throughout the Bible, throughout cultures, even the Pagan cultures had "divorce." Why? Because there must have been some sort of an agreement that must be broken for a divorce, how it happens is debatable fair enough.

## Protect your soul, get married

It must happen if you do not want to be living in sin, and so I would share that with your son and with the young lady that this is what the Bible teaches about the subject. If you are not in that sort of relationship and you are sleeping with that woman, you're sinning, and, therefore, you are in danger. Your soul is in danger, and you're in danger of judgment at the church and eternal levels, so please get married now.

Here's the one that I hear regularly, but everything I have is yours. That thing is, "What we've been married for so long, we love each other, and we love it in the state recognizes it." Anyway, so it's not a big deal, and then if that's the case, then dude, the formal ceremony and whether it is in the eyes of God or not, God's eyes are on it, and it's valid. So, if they want to do something secular, fine, but if you want your son, who may or may not be a Christian, not to be willfully sinning against God, they don't need to get married. idea I'd wretched.org idea at wretched.org former COVID patient what have you got I got an easy one from you from before you from Vicki you were never coveted yeah what do you eat.

## Many of us want perfection in the church

Applied to this situation, many of us want perfection in the church. We do, and that's a desire, frankly, but it becomes ill-advised for our zeal for righteousness. You Google that; you'll find the article. Calvin really said, "Ultimately, because God so desires unity and because his understanding of holiness was very practical, he understood that even though we're called "Saints" we're not yet, and therefore an assembling of people who are not that holy, you are going to have unholy results. That means no church is going to be perfect. It is a process, not just in your personal sanctification but in sanctification as a group in the local body." Then Calvin went on to say, "As long as the essentials are there of word and sacrament church discipline, as long as the word is rightly preached, no heresy sacraments of baptism Lord supper. They're being administered, and there's church discipline that occasionally takes place when necessary. You don't have any great reason to leave that church. Now that doesn't mean you can't.

## Looking for perfection

It's because you're looking for perfection; you've got a false understanding. Could it be because of your circumstances or your zip code? You don't have a lot of options or any options at all if those three criteria are being met. Not only should you stay on Calvin, but you also throw yourself into the work of that church. You commit to it.

"Oh, but no, I don't want people to know I go there."

Throw yourself into it and serve. That is the only way anybody is going to start getting healthier. If you contribute to it, can there ever be some reasons or programs and those issues? Yes, but they should be worked out with your pastor, and if the baton can't be handed off to another pastor gracefully.

## What does the Bible say about marriage?

I said the Bible is the one that you need to follow. School is one that we need to follow, which is why even though we have other examples we will take in our society today, the main idea is from the Bible. We're going to use some verses from Genesis, First Corinthians, and Ephesians. All these verses we're going to use to get you all the information you need to have for a successful marriage. What does the Bible say about marriage?

Hey everyone, I'm Mark Mapei from God's work.com. A place where we apply the Bible to our life. In this episode, we will talk about seven things the Bible says about marriage. We're going to go through these points pretty quickly, so I'm not going to list out all the Bible verses because

## Marriage was created by God

We'd be here for hours, but if you want to do a more in-depth study on this topic, if you want to check what the Bible says about marriage, it is that marriage was created by God and is good. So, God created humans in his image, so it shouldn't be a surprise that God gave humans ingenuity and the ability to create and think of things and then bring them into existence, so to speak. The idea of governments, the way society should be structured, or certain cultural practices, humans can create certain things because God's given us the ability to do that. Here's the thing with marriage it wasn't an idea created by man.

## A biblical principle that was right at the beginning of creation, for example, Genesis 2:24

We thought an instituted marriage was a biblical principle that was right at the beginning of creation. For example, Genesis 22:4 says, "Therefore a man shall leave his father and mother and hold fast to his wife, and they shall become one flesh." So, you see, in that passage, it doesn't say that a man shall leave his father and mother and join a woman, and then they create marriage. Down the line, it says, so, you see right there that God is actually the author of marriage. It also says that marriage is good. Everything God created is good; for example,

Proverbs 18:22 says, "He who finds a wife finds a good thing and the same." Obviously goes for women who find a husband they find a good thing in marriage.

## Bible says that marriage was created by God

Bible says that marriage was created by God and is good. The second thing that the Bible says about marriage is that it's something not just for Christians but for the whole world. I know it's a Christian idea, which originated with God, but God created this for the whole world. For example, in Genesis 1:28, God is speaking to humans, where he says, "I'm creating you to be fruitful and multiply and to rule and subdue the earth."

So marriage is not just an institution just for Christians. God wants all people who are called to marriage to join in the marriage covenant and bond with one another, and you can see this in the benefit it brings to societies. Study after study shows that when traditional marriage isn't emphasized in a society, that society starts breaking down. So there are many benefits between having a dad and a mom helping raise kids together.

## Christian's experience redeeming quality

It's just super beneficial because God created it that way. The idea of marriage falls under the theological doctrine of "common grace." Not every person on earth has God's special grace or saving grace, which is when we understand and receive and put our faith in Jesus Christ to have a relationship with God through the gospel. That's a certain type of saving grace that only Christians experience, but there's another form of grace the Bible refers to as "common grace," and what that means is everything good in creation, the food we eat, the water we drink, the air we breathe, the sunshine, the crops, everything that is good is from God, and that's common great. So, even if the unbelievers don't give God the recognition He deserves for good in their life, the Bible says all that is from God. Therefore, a marriage falls under the principle of common grace given to the entire world.

## God does not want Christians to marry non-Christians

While the Bible says that marriage is for Christians and non-Christians, the Bible specifically says it should not be between an unbeliever and a believer. The Bible calls this unequally yoked, so the Bible says that God does not want Christians to marry non-Christians. It says that in first Corinthians 6, verses 14 through 15, and 1st Corinthians 7, verse 39, the fourth thing the Bible says about marriage is that it's supposed to be between one man and one woman. Every type of example you see in marriage points to this specific type of marriage.

## God created marriage to avoid polygamy

It's the only marriage that God ordains and has talked about in his word. This means that there are two things that are for sure a sin in God's eyes. "Polygamy" means that there's more than one man and one woman in the marriage. That is a sin. Now you might think of the Old Testament, where there are certain characters like King David and Solomon and all these other guys who actually had multiple wives, and that is absolutely true. But nowhere in the Bible are you going to find that God was condoning that or commanding that is something that they did on their own.

## Marriage is between one man and one woman (no Gay marriage before God's eyes)

God has always said to marry one woman. Also, since the Bible clearly says that marriage is between one man and one woman, this means that gay marriage is something that's not in the Bible and is a sin because it's endorsing homosexuality which again is a violation of the way God originally created humans to be paired to a husband and a wife those are some loaded statements. I just said that it is a unique bond between a husband and a wife. It says in genesis 22:4 again that a man shall leave his father and mother and be joined to his wife and become one flesh.

## The Bible says premarital sex is a sin. What God has joined together, let no man separate

You see an intimate relationship within the Bible. It's always paired with commitment and intimacy in the scriptures. That's why premarital sex is a sin in the Bible because you're having an extreme form of intimacy without the extreme form of commitment in the covenant of marriage. Premarital sex I think, is pretty clear for most Christians, and they know that it's wrong. There's also a danger in having an emotional intimacy that crosses the line or cohabitation with someone of the opposite sex, and emotional intimacy is two things that should be, again, reserved for the marriage. Next, the Bible says that what God has joined together, man should not separate. In other words, divorce is not honored in the scriptures except for one thing;

an actual sexual affair. So, even when an affair happens within the marriage, the Bible doesn't command a divorce. But it does allow for it.

## The Bible says that marriage is a symbolic representation of the relationship between Christ and the Church

Lastly, the Bible says that marriage symbolizes the relationship between Christ and the Church. Ephesians 5, verses 22 through 33, says that the husband represents Christ and the wife represents the Church; that's why a husband and a wife are equally important in the relationship, but they do play different roles. A husband is supposed to lead and love his family, and a wife is supposed to love and support that leadership which you can see in the relationship between Christ and the Church. Christ is ultimately our leader, and the Church is following Christ and honoring him, so marriage is such a unique and special relationship that God uses. Those are the main principles. God's view for marriage is very and God is the all other the guidance to marriage which is just what this book is about.

We want to make sure we give you all the ingredients, all the verses that are necessary.

## Marriage is between a man and a woman. A man and a woman are married in God's eyes when they have completed some kind of formal wedding

Nowhere explicitly states at what point God considers a man and a woman to be married. The Bible's silence on the matter of identifying the moment a man and one woman are married in God's eyes is a complex undertaking. Here are the 3 most common views. First, God only considers a man and a woman married when they are legally married; that is when they become husband and wife. Second, a man and a woman are married in God's eyes when they have completed some kind of formal wedding. Both are all being wow. Third, gotten sensors there's a man and woman to be married at the moment they engage in sexual intercourse. Let's look at each of the three views, and your strengths and weakness is a breach. First, God only can consider there's a man and a woman married when they are Mary the subscript social support typically given for this view is the command to the governmental laws 13 versus one through seven and first Peter chapter 2 verse 17.

## The marriage needs a contract signed by both parties in order to be legally enforceable

The argument is that if the government requires certain procedures and paperwork before your marriage is recognized, then people should submit themselves to that process. It is definitely only biblical for people to submit to the government as long as the required amendments do not contradict God's word and are reasonable.

Romans chapter 13, verses one and 2:22, tells us that everyone must submit himself to the governing authorities, for there is no authority except that which God has established. The authorities that exist have been established by God.

## Marriage regulations around the world today

He who rebels against authority is rebelling against what God has instituted. Doing so will bring judgment on themselves. However, there are some weaknesses and potential problems with this view. First, major marriage churches existed before any government was organized. For years, people were getting married with no such thing or space set. Even today, there are some countries that have no governmental recognition of marriage and no legal requirements. Third, there are some governments that place requirements 4/4 is legally recognized as an example. Some countries require waiting, which seems to be held in the Church 22 teachings and overseen by a leader. Obviously, for those who have strong disagreements with the Church and the Church's understanding of marriage as an institution created by God,

## Marriage, according to the Bible, is a man and a woman married in God's eyes

It would be unbiblical to submit to being married for the church folks to make the legitimacy of the marriage union solely dependent on the government. Mental status is the indirectly same thing as Tory's definition of marriage, which may fluctuate. The second common viewpoint of what constitutes marriage according to the Bible is that a man and woman are married in God's eyes when they have completed some kind of formal wedding. Some interpreters understand God bringing Adam and Eve in Genesis chapter two, verse 20, as God overseeing.

## Every Greek culture in the history of humanity has seen some kind of formal wedding. John chapter 22; Jesus was present at a wedding ceremony

The first ceremony of the modern practice is of a father giving away his daughter to a man in a wedding ceremony. John Chapter 22; Jesus attended a wedding ceremony. Jesus just would not have attended such an event if he did not approve. Jesus is present since adding the wedding ceremony by no means shows God's ceremony, but it does not dictate that the wedding ceremony is acceptable in God's sight. Every Greek culture in the history of humanity has seen some kind of formal wedding ceremony. In every culture, there is an event and action hub Inette about are proclamation that is recognized as declaring people to be married. The third common viewpoint is that God cannot consider sitters. There is a man and a woman to be married now. They engage in sexual intercourse, and there are some.

## Every married couple is not truly married in God's eyes

Who takes this? That's mean. Every married couple is not truly married in God's eyes. Others are any that have sex. There is the two of them to be married. The basis for this view is the fact that sexual intercourse between husband and wife is the ultimate fulfillment, in Genesis chapter 2 verse 20

In this sentence, sexual intercourse is the final seal of the name marriage church covenant. However, the view that intercourse consents to marriage is not biblically sound. If the couple is legally and ceremonially married but, for some reason, is unable to engage in sexual intercourse, that couple is still considered married. We know that God does not equate sexual intercourse with marriage.

## The difference between a real wife from a concubine 2 chronicles Chapter 11 verse 20

Based on the fact that the Old Testament often distinguishes a real wife from a concubine. For example, second chronicle, Chapter 11, verse 20 and 11 describes 11 King's family life. Rehoboam loved the daughter of Absalon more than any of his other wives and concubines, he can't get 11 wives, and 6,663 concubines in this first verse concubines, who had sexual intercourse with the king are not considered why mentioned as a separate category. Also, so first percent 17 verse two indicates that sex before marriage is immorality if sexual intercourse causes this a couple to become married.

## Example of a couple being married solely by sexual intercourse without a wedding ceremony

It could not be considered moral as the couple would be considered married. Now that they have engaged in sexual intercourse, there is absolutely no basis for an unmarried couple to have sex and then declare themselves to be married. They are thereby declaring all futures for sexual relations to be moral and God honoring some point to genesis chapter 20:24 and the story of Isaac and Rebecca as an example of a couple being married solely by sexual intercourse without a wedding ceremony.

## Marriage today versus marriage in ancient times

Marriage today versus marriage in ancient times. We can still see marriage in genesis, and marriage is taught in Bible means when we're going to come and make it different because we already talk about it because male marriage we can though it's by Its biblical, but we have to see the policies we're living by now in the whole world. We're living now oh marriage today because we just talk about, even given. Marriage is not something we can talk about because the Bible doesn't allow a man to marry another man or a woman to marry another woman. That means, according to our lecture or according to our book, everything we think is from the Bible. We're not going to send anything that is not far from God, spoken by God. Marriage is an institution that was instituted by God, so this is what we're talking about today, and when I want to make sure with the book.

## The things we talk about are how to make your marriage better and better every day

We are writing for you, to give you everything that you need about marriage, especially for those unbelievers or believers. But we give more than that because we help you understand the concept. If you're going to get married, if you are going to get married or if you already been married, how you can resolve some problem. how can you make your marriage better and better every day. These are the things we're talking about but not how we are going to quickly give the difference from the in the initiation to today day marriage these are different. That we that we're going to make that are very important.

## Isaac and Rebecca were married with no certificate or paperwork, so how should Christians define marriage today

For some, marriage is a challenging time. Isaac and Rebecca, for example, simply entered it to attend, and then they were married with no certificate or pain or paperwork, so how should Christians define marriage?

Today's Christians should define marriage the same way it's been defined by the Bible for thousands of years ago. It's been "a man leaves his father and his mother and becomes joined to his wife in the flesh. marriage damage then. That is the covenant relationship between them. Between a man and a woman before God, before God, and Jesus, in fact, is this stuff ignition nation imagine. He quotes Genesis's account of marriage because he believes that it is still valid. Then he adds his own calm commentary, saying what they are before God and what is joined together, let no one separate. In other words, Jesus believes marriage is a God-ordained institution, and so when Isaac and Rebecca got married, they made a committed commitment to each other, which is recorded in Genesis 20.

## They made a committed commitment to each other that is recorded in Genesis 20

When the Bible says, "Isaac brought Rebecca Becky into the 10th," well, that's just the rector's reference to them consummating the marriage church. It's true there is no mention of a certificate or paperwork, and never to a four-hour house. Why? Because marriage is an institution of God, not the invention of the state, and that's why no legal documents are needed. When I got married to the most glorious, by the way, we exchanged our vows and were in front of our pastor and our friends and family.

## Marriage commitment to each other before God (vow)

Most importantly, we made our commitment to each other before God, for God. Now some type of time later that day, my wife filled out the necessary paperwork to register our marriage with the state, but that's a subsequent certificate we got from the government. It does not make us any more married when we exchange our wedding vow before God, for God. Our mirror marriage began again, and then at the church marriage. As you can see, this is a pre-political institution and existed long before the state. If you've got something, don't say they put it in the comment, but I am not your lawyer. If you need some legal advice by specific to dictate to your situation, you need the lawyer you're up with in your area. When we talk about the topic of marriage, you have to that the laws are different in every state, so you want to make sure to pay the fine into the little of your resource.

## You must go through what is called solemnization

We're going to hit the highlight of the wall. That's generally only applicable in most jurisdictions. Now, the requirements to get married in 2023; number 1, you need to get a marriage license in 2023. You have to go through what's called "solemnization." Kind of a tricky working word. It just basically means "a space," so let's talk about the license issue. First, you need to go to the county clerk in whatever county you're in. That is in charge of issuing the marriage license, and there are certain qualifications and there are things that you need to get one. When you go, you know, you want to take your ID. That's important. Then bring a little bit of money because these things aren't for free, so the clerks are going to make you and your spouse say swear here with your right hand and swear where to steps the firm can you do whatever you do.

## What should I do about my spouse or partner with a nonbeliever

I guess it doesn't really matter what we think. Biblically, what should I do about my spouse or partner with a nonbeliever, and this is something that definitely must be dealt with correctly. My story is long, and really complicated. Sometimes throughout, maybe some of these videos or all of them kind of get strung out through it.

# Testimony of an "Unbeliever" converted to Christian Life

I was saved at the age of 30, I was up voicing as an unbeliever, an atheist. I do all the lingo of patriotism, and I purported that ideology pretty much like a preacher of atheism, but that was what I had confirmed that I believed. That's what Stephanie was dealing with for the first 7-8 years of our relationship, but I've done destruction, strung out on hard drugs with a very big anger problem and very low self-esteem, and suffer from depression and anxiety. Everything that goes with that sort of lifestyle, so that was what she was dealing with. So I think the first turning point in which I saw God's way apart in our lives was when we got pregnant because of our first child.

## Nonbeliever's testimony

I had a voice that said I don't think I can do this. I didn't. The first year was really a honeymoon, a puppy love period. It was love at first sight, and I didn't know who he was, but I knew that he was an alcoholic. I didn't realize the severity of how bad of an alcoholic he was until years into our relationship. So she was not prepared in any way. No support on any ankle with how to deal with it. No street 83 stops, 3 sport athletes, goody two shoes, and so anyway, when I started to realize, "wow, he really has problems; alcohol problem, anger problems, like to fight, I don't think that this is the person I want to be with." Then we found out we were pregnant with our first child. I just thought at the first instance that Stephanie was going to leave me, and we were held together by something because I wouldn't separate from my child. There was no option for abortion. That was not ever in our vocabulary, and that's not to say that we're better than others. I just want to say that was not our option. Problems presented to us from either of our April, and I was not going to abandon my child or myself in pursuit of alcohol. Tragically I ended up just tagging along with her and carrying all the alcoholism. That was when we found out I was pregnant. I cried, and he was joyful and excited. He was like, "we're going to be OK."

## Nonbeliever details

I wasn't so sure because I didn't want to be with you. You have an alcohol problem, but I really felt God nudged at my heart and said, "No, just watch," you know, and so I went through it and had a beautiful baby boy. You know, years passed, and we were hanging on. We had the whole time, so these years passed. We refer to these as the dark ones. It was bad. I'm not going to go into detail; it would take a very long time. The story is very intricate. It's a lot of details that we could cover in it.

All of a sudden, from that point, something clicked because I became a good guy. That's not what happened. No, he continued to struggle with alcohol, and unknowing of me, he was a meth user, and I didn't know that. Well, fast forward, and I was gone. He had moments of sobriety and tried very hard on his own to be sober. 12-step programs and with A.

## Always believing in God

I have my own right to those, but I went to Iraq. When I got home, well, Iraq almost broke him. I mean, I was at this point where I was falling apart.

My life was falling apart; it was terrible. I was looking back, and I was 20 something-year-old man who had no goals, no expectations, no hope, came from nowhere, had nobody, had nothing, and I couldn't keep myself together.

It seemed like every time I turned around, I was doing something, and it was always me. I never made it, I never had school, but I was always making my own turmoil and dragging Stephanie.

Now this time, hunter along with. So at this point, Stephanie was done. She should be. That was a tiring long time to put up with somebody else. She believed in God this whole time.

## Jesse's salvation story

So when I got home from Iraq is when we got married. I thought we were married, and now things will be different back home from Iraq. We had passed a really big test in our relationship, and even after one year into our marriage, nothing had changed. He continued to drink a lot, he continued to use meth, and that's when I really was done. I packed his bags, and I wanted nothing to do with them. I was over this lifestyle of his, and that's when Jesse's salvation story kind of begins.

But before we kind of go over it, exactly what weekend but? So how did I get through it? Here's what it is, "Praying." So I grew up not being protestant, and I'll be honest, I learned nothing as not being protestant; I've learned more. I'm 30, almost 35 years old, and I've learned more about true Christianity and the Bible and who Jesus really is in the past five years than I had during the first 30 years. The first time that Jesse and I met to the time that he was saved, was an 8 years gap. And through that, I was praying a lot, but I was praying for things. Like, "Oh Lord, please let Jesse stop drinking." "Lord! Let him stop doing drugs," "Lord! Let him stop flirting with girls!" I was praying these things that were going to be beneficial for me, you know, if he stopped drinking, I do not have to deal with him being, you know, angry and drunk, and they were genuine.

They were prayed toward him, but they were selfish prayers. This is a very good couple, and this is a very good example of a believer, and then that man is the unbeliever husband. So this is what we are listening to, or this is what we are writing.

This story is a true story, and it's a wild story about the lady speaking with her husband and explaining the situation because this is a real-life story. She's a Christian. She knows Jesus. She's a Christian, we're talking about a believer, and the man was an unbeliever. Someone that lived like, "if those things magically went away, my life would be easier."

## Jesse came home after I packed his bags and said give me one more chance. (Conversion)

It wasn't until I was ready to leave him that I had his bags packed. We had been married a year ago; we had been together for eight years. It wasn't the reason you don't pray for somebody's problems because that's not it. No. It came to drinking; that wasn't the problem. Addiction and anything that went along with it, the girls or whatever, the horrible lifestyle was not the problem. I mean, that's just the product of the underlying problem. It was where we started going to church. Jesse came home after I packed his bags and said, “Give me one more chance again; I came home asking for one more chance.” I had no idea that stuff was at the end of her rope, I had no idea that she had my stuff packed, I had no idea.

## Someone might not be a Christian, but that does not mean they cannot have good behavior

I was in jeopardy of losing my family, but I was coming back home after nine days. Fastpitch that. I had to eat, and I was in the Burger King parking lot. I said to myself.

This is a real-life story. Her husband and everything we are listening to or everything we are writing is a real-life story of two couples. The lady was a Christian, and the man, the husband, was an unbeliever.

Don't, Stephanie. I'm hurting people around me that I don't deserve. It’s OK. I stop here because I want to make sure I don't put too much stuff in my book because, you know, when someone is not a believer, is not a Christian, it doesn't mean they do all the bad things in the world. That means some of them are not believers, but that doesn't mean they don’t know anything about the law.

## Christians do not marry nonchristians

This is not where I'm going to be. This is what I want. This is not what I want to talk about, and I don't want to talk about people that are doing all the things in life because they are not Christians. This is not what I'm doing.

This book talks about people that are Christian and those that are not Christian. You are not a Christian, or you are a Christian; this is not what we want to talk about. We want to see someone that is a christian and can lead the order that is not Christian, to the Christian faith, and to salvation. This is what we're talking about here, so that is why we are going to anyways in most of this story because we don't want to talk about some deeper issue in society. This is not what this book is about. So if you see we

## Have a marriage ministry

We have God's perspective of your marriage and relationship and are just going into it. For this first one, I wanted to share a brief story of testimony we heard years ago, when we were going to have a marriage ministry, of this couple. We're sharing from the stage their testimony of what Christ did in their relationship and how God moved them in their marriage, and do you want to share a little bit from what you heard from the stage that night?

Well, I remember that the husband was going through an extreme level of things that I've struggled with. Then he went even further in actually having relationships with prostitutes and turned into just a totally disgusting, destroyed, broken person married to a woman who loves God. They were both Christians, but one gave himself over to sin and depravity. Their testimony on how she walked with this man was inspirational and truly showed the gospel. It was so powerful. I remember sitting there and the pastor asking her the next question, "how did you do it?"

## I had to see him as a brother in Christ, she said

"How did you endure those years of him walking through that sin and remaining faithful to him?" She said, "I knew in my heart that I had to see him as a brother in Christ, and I had to see him as Christ sees him. He needed salvation; he needed to believe in who God was," and she was convinced that his heart and his salvation were more important than anything else. That was such an impactful story. I still remember it to this day, and when I hear those stories of redemption and reconciliation of a totally broken marriage, and you're like, how could like when we heard it, it's like, man, I don't know how I would deal with that. Everybody was crying in the audience. Everybody just realized the power of God in people's lives when they let God work when they have a heavenly perspective. You're just saying that when we have God's perspective because, in those situations, as I said, all of us are thinking, "I don't know if I could do that." It's because we only have this one real conversation about how to live with an unbelieving spouse perspective, and our president is like, "I would never want to walk in that."

## God's perspective for our marriage

Right, well, I think too. When it comes to our perspectives, I want you to love me, I want my spouse to love me, and I want to be able to love them. I don't want to suffer, and if we have God's perspective, we realize

God loves our spouse more than even we do, and I think that it's really important to know that God loves our spouse. God loves their hearts and wants their hearts and desires that a husband and wife chase after him together. That's God's perspective. A wrong perspective to have, one we've heard this time and time again, is, "Oh, God wants me to be happy, therefore, I'm just going to leave my spouse, and you know what, God does want us to have joy."

## God wants me to be happy

His intention for us is not our happiness; it's our holiness. It's our maturity and growth. It's our obedience, and so have the perspective that God wants me to be happy. You know what's going to happen in your life? You're always going to be running away from things that are hard. Yeah, because you're like, "well, God doesn't want that for me; he wants me to only be happy."

You have many things in life that are difficult, and God wants those for us, so it's hard for us if we have that perspective of just God. First of all, it's not biblical. It's wrong. But if we have that perspective, we're never going to pursue what God wants. We're always going to be running to comfort, and you know there are a lot of things in life that God has us walk through and others that are uncomfortable for us. They mature as they grow, they give us perseverance, and they give us hope for a future. This is what the Bible talks about, and so the heavenly perspective, the godly perspective, recognizes that God has something to be done in our marriage.

## God cares about my spouse, and he wants us to be happy. He wants me to walk out of my life a certain way, to be a ministry in my home

He cares about my spouse more than I do, and he wants me to walk out of my life a certain way to be a ministry in my home. That's the perspective we need to have. The Bible says what God says. How can I shift my mind off? That woman who decided that I needed to start seeing my husband in this way. She changed her perspective from "my marriage is falling apart, my husband doesn't love me, my husband's cheating on me" to "my husband's all things that are true." Reason to having every reason to walk away, and she changed her perspective like "I'm not going to see him as I was before; I'm going to see him now as a brother who needs Jesus."

## She did say she set boundaries in that relationship, but she did not stop loving him. She did not stop praying for him and preaching to him

The truth of the word, and I'm going to start praying for him. I will start loving him in that way. Now, I also remember she did say she set boundaries in that relationship, but she didn't stop loving him. She didn't stop praying for him and preaching to him and encouraging him, and asking the Holy Spirit to change him. One of the points that we have down for having a godly perspective is that your marriage is a ministry.

So can you share a little bit about what that looks like, what that means, that "your marriage is a ministry?" "What does that mean for a husband and a wife?"

Well, the base level of what "our marriage is ministry" means is that in many of our marriages, the right didn't create them; that is the symbol they represent; the wife represents the "Church."

## The husband stands for Christ, and that is the symbol of that marriage

The husband represents Christ, and that's the symbol of that marriage. What did Christ come to do? He came to reconcile the Church to the father, right? He came to heal the church; he came to forgive the church and to be a sacrifice for the church. You see, this relationship of Christ sacrificing himself for a cheating, lying, abusive, and you know, a destructive church, a body of people, and he redeems them. You see, instead of him leaving, divorcing, and throwing them to the side, we're not walking out with the father called him to do. He comes for them, dies for them, and reconciles them to the father still, and that's what he does for us. That's the gospel. Like, Oh yeah, while we were still sinners.

## That he reconciled me, that he is given me the Holy Spirit, and so you have the symbol of marriage being a symbol of the gospel, Jesus Christ, and the Church

He died for us. He forgave me, he's reconciled me, he's given me the Holy Spirit, and so you have the symbol of marriage being a symbol of the gospel, Christ and the Church, and what that means is that it is in itself a ministry. It is that when you are walking out rightly in a mature, biblical, and godly marriage, you're representing the gospel to the world, and by and through every interaction that you have with your spouse, you are through forgiveness, love, grace and sharing all these things with your spouse, you're actually showing them the father heart of God. Like you are being that ministry of reconciliation where you're drawing them closer to God through the way that you're reconciling. That's part of the ministry; your marriage being your first ministry means the first place you minister, the 1st place you preach the gospel, the 1st place you love and protect, and the 1st place you serve in your marriage is to your spouse. Yeah, you know, I serve you, love you, and preach the gospel to you.

## Minister in your home

I wash you in the word, as for Ephesians 5. Now I'm 25, tell me what to do, and that's my first ministry. I cannot neglect this ministry to my wife and go and fulfill another ministry, right? So when it comes to you being in a marriage with an unbelieving spouse, that will be the first person you're going to be preaching to.

Well, this doesn't mean you can't be doing ministry elsewhere. You know for certain that your Church or an orphanage or you know whatever

God's given you as a ministry in your life, that you're just gifted in, but your spouse is the person that God wants you to minister, today and every day, with the way you are at home, with how you talk. We're going to get to a subscription that talks about that, but your spouse, your unbelieving spouse, is the first person that you're called to minister to. It's good OK, so moving on to #2, you're going to share a little bit more about this, but don't leave, yeah.

## He goes to the people that are unequally yoked

We just talked about the beauty of that story. That husband and wife, the husband who is just totally broken, totally just running away from his wife and treating her not the way a husband should be treating her, and she took it from the Holy Spirit to be like, "Oh, this is my ministry," and instead of leaving when she probably could have when no one would have judged her, she stayed. I just want to read this in first Corinthians Chapter 7, verse 12; it's a few scriptures, and I'm going to pull out a few things from this. It's just to the rest, I say so. I'll step back a little bit and a few verses. Really, he's talking to Christian marriages that are equally yoked and but then he goes to the people that are unequally yoked.

## A woman has a husband who is an unbeliever, and he can sense to live with her, she should not divorce him

He says to the rest, "I say, I, not the Lord, that if any brother has a wife who is an unbeliever and she can sense to live with him, he should not divorce her. If any woman has a husband who is an unbeliever and he can sense to live with her, she should not divorce him, for the unbelieving husband is made holy because of his wife and the unbelieving wife is made holy because of her husband. Otherwise, your children would be unclean, but as it is, they are holy. However, if the unbelieving partner separates, let it be, so in such cases, the brother or sister is not enslaved. God has called you to peace, for how do you know wife whether you will save your husband or how do you know husband whether you will save your wife?

## Now suddenly, the holy spirits come into the world. Jesus Christ on the cross and people are getting saved

First of all, the fact that this is in the Bible that Paul is like, "Hey, actually, I'm going to talk to those believers who have a husband or a wife who aren't believers." Do you know why this is here? Because up until this point, there existed a law in the Jewish culture that you would not marry outside of the Jewish culture, that you wouldn't intermarry. A lot was unheard of. You were unclean if you did so, but now all of a sudden, the holy spirits come into the world. Jesus Christ is out on the cross, and people are getting saved left and right.

## To the rest of you who have come to the Lord and your spouse has not. This is how you should live, but he says so. He says if your unbelieving spouse does not want to leave meaning, you are to marry

It was common at this point for a woman or a man to come to the Lord, apart from their husband, and then they get home, and their husband or wife is not a believer. It wasn't like they were all coming together to the Lord; that probably happened in a lot of cases, but you have this often and Paul saying, "Actually, I'm going to say to the rest of you who have come to the Lord and your spouse, this is how you should live," but he says so he says if your unbelieving spouse doesn't want to leave meaning you're married, and they realize you're a Christian they're like oh you're you believe in Jesus you're going to follow Jesus, and they say like OK.

## If the unbeliever wants to leave, let him or her do so

I still love you. Let's do this, and there's still an unbeliever, but they don't want to leave you crossing, like "don't leave" like stay there, what do you feel like he's saying stay there? Well, I love it. Is it expected at the end because it's like that? I have that big old question of the future how do you know what if you help bring that person to the Lord? Well, think about it this is the marriage relationship, this binding of two bodies, the same household being this same home, under the same roof, forever, right? Like every day after day, hour after hour.

## You are preaching the gospel to them every single day. You are loving them, you are encouraging them, you are praying for them

It is the perfect environment to preach the gospel. Your spouse, that is, the unbelieving spouse, cannot leave, especially if they want to be there. With your life and your actions, and your efforts, you are preaching the gospel to them every single day. You are loving them, you are encouraging them, you are praying for them, and they are like, "This woman is a different woman; this man is a different man."

Yes, it is a perfect setup. I think of the movie, yes. I think of the movie "Case for Christ." Well, that's a good movie. At least trouble right, and his wife comes to the Lord, and she just starts praying for him and living out the Christian life in front of him and never leaves him even though she's just crying out to Lord. Lord changes his heart. Why is it like this? Why does he struggle? He didn't want to leave right away, but like sort of, if you don't change, I'm out of her, and you know what happened? He came to the Lord. This is a true story. He came to Lord because of his wife and her persistence in walking out the gospel as a believer, and that is what this book says. Don't leave because who knows if you're unbelieving wife or husband will or won't get saved because of your life.

## Who knows, husbands, if your unbelieving wife will not get saved because of your life

Who knows, wife, if you believe the husband could say, "Because of your life, I just think that is so beautiful that God thought it didn't think about he knew it was important to put this in here so that we weren't floundering like well I don't know how I'm supposed to do this so. I love that you brought up that story of lee Strobel and how his wife was praying for him because our next point is "pray for them and pray for yourself." So it's really important that we. That's called an example, and so if you are a believer, if you love the Lord, and your spouse is not the most powerful thing, what you can do in their life is to live out what the Bible calls you to live out which is to be a Christian in front of them, to them, for them, with them. Their subscriptions are going to reinitiate. The Bible tells us exactly what kind of example we could be and how powerful it is. In first Corinthians, at the very end, it says how do you know wife whether you will save your husband or how do you know husband whether you will save your wife?

## Your example could potentially save your spouse.

This is literally saying, like you being in proximity in the marriage and remaining in the marriage, that your life could potentially, and your example could potentially save your spouse, so why don't you read those scriptures? I'm your set of scriptures. I'm going to start with first Peter three, one through 2, w says, likewise wives be subject to your own husband so that if some do not obey the word, they may be one without a word by the conduct of their wives when they see your respectful and pure conduct. So, this is a really powerful verse, and I just love that this verse is in here because it's just encouragement to the wife's heart; you know, earlier, we talked about endurance.

## Because you are practicing righteousness before your spouse.

And enduring the weight of having an unbelieving spouse, and there's power here in the way that we can conduct ourselves according to scripture according to God's word. Scripture calls for us to exhibit respectful and pure conduct, which means living out our beliefs with integrity and purity, particularly in our relationships with unbelieving spouses. And it says right here that they may be one without a word like you don't even need to go into explaining why you're doing the things that you're doing, although if they ask, I mean by all means, give them the answer because it's powerful but God saying it's your contact that's going to reveal it. Because the reality is you couldn't potentially you couldn't in reality

## I should say speak to your spouse 24/7 about what the word says enter and convince them to become a Christian that actions are so powerful.

Speak to your spouse 24/7 about what the word says and convince them to become a Christian that actions are so powerful. Still, they will see your actions every day, so again, if you say one thing and do another right; they will never believe you. They're not going to see it as they're not going to your life isn't going to betray the truth of what you say is true. But when you say things to them, you know the reason. I believe what the Bible says because 'You know what God's done in my life, and this is what I believe in Jesus. Then when I see you back that way, when they see you walk that way, they'll be like, whoa, you know I can't stop this. What's happening? Why does this person love me so much, especially when I treat them this way or when I don't believe what they believe or so. Even though this is specifically talking to the wives and in her role and the way she can walk out the gospel in her marriage to an unbelieving spouse or an or a spouse that's not obeying the word because we talked about in the beginning right so it could be an unbelieving spouse or it could be totally disobedient like that one husband at the beginning of our or you know this episode, but the principle can still work that.

## We treat our spouses the way the Bible tells us to treat them.

We treat our spouse the way the Bible tells us to treat them when we walk out of this Gospel, and it actually, later on in verse seven, says how a husband can treat his wife. If you want to read that for sure, it says, likewise, husbands live with their wives in an understanding way showing honor to the woman as the weaker vessel since they're heirs with you of the grace of life so that your prayers may not be hindered. So again, this is some people might think this verse is controversial but

## The husband recognizes, like Oh my gosh, I am going to walk with my wife in an understanding way. I am going to show her that I understand her. I am going to work to teach her and love her.

I find it beautiful when a husband commits to walking with his wife in understanding, showing her love, and working on learning about her. This aligns with the Biblical command in Ephesians 5:25

for husbands to love their wives as Christ loves the church. If you look at the gospel, the husband represents Christ in the marriage and is sacrificial in his love for her and wash her still in the word. Even if she doesn't share his beliefs, he can still live out those biblical roles and commands as a Christian husband to an unbelieving wife. The husband can walk with his wife in understanding, recognizing that they both share in the grace of life. As discussed earlier, this requires a godly perspective as a commitment to supporting one's spouse. And so you know even though Jennifer and

**We are supposed to look at the world; we do not look at it through just our own opinions or even through just our own experiences.**

I have never personally experienced this, but we don't have to rely solely on our own opinions or experiences to understand the world. The word of God provides guidance on how we should view the world. Our personal experiences may be biased and lead us to think in ways that are not in line with biblical teachings. The Bible is unchanging and inherently provides a clear framework for understanding the world. And I think it's beautiful that God knew that we would need this guide on how to interact within a marriage where there's an unequally yoked relationship. Lastly, the most beautiful part about this is none of this has anything to do with just having a happy marriage, right? Like it's not just about, you know, being healthy and happy and joyful and like, 'oh as long if my husband got saved, you know things would be much better, which they would be, but we have hardships.

## Believers, you know, so the point is not just to have a comfortable, happy marriage, the point is to be holy, and the point is the salvation of your spouse's soul is the most important thing.

In our marriage, as believers, we understand that a comfortable and happy marriage is not the ultimate goal. The point is to be holy, and the point is this the salvation of your spouse's soul is the most important thing. This is why Christ came to the world. It is what God's doing in the world as he's through Christ reconciling people to himself that we would have eternity with him right so as we've given all this encouragement to a spouse who may be married to an unbeliever or someone who isn't walking that way what would you say to the person listening to us right now who is that spouse who's unbelieving or maybe isn't walking in obedience to God's word so.

## It's true that Jesus came to save us. He reconciles us with the father so we can have a great relationship with him. Without Jesus, we can't save ourselves.

First of all, I would say repent and believe in the Lord Jesus. It's true that Jesus came to save us and reconcile us with the father so we can have the right relationship with him. Without Jesus, we can't save ourselves. We need a savior to be renewed, regenerated, and filled with the Holy Spirit that he's promised us. The Holy Spirit will empower us to walk in freedom, strength, and authority.

## You should believe today that you love so much that they would share the gospel that they want you to be saved.

If you don't believe in Gospel that your loved ones share with you, you should still believe in the Lord Jesus. So that you would be in heaven with them one day that's our goal is that we want to be an eternity with our father in heaven and not eternal separation from him. That's the truth, that's the gospel, and it's a good gospel. It's called the good news and the reason for hope. I mean, I don't know how other people do it in this world without the saving knowledge of Christ because with it in our lives and the hardships that we've endured, there is hope, there's a future, and we are just we're excited about it. It fuels us. Yeah, and no matter what happens in this life, like I said, it's not just about comfortable, or you know, happily ever after; it's about eternal hope. Yeah because man

## Rejoice in persecution. People who believe in Jesus rejoice because of the hope they have and so, like I said, this gospel is not just that we would have a happy, comfortable life now, but that we have eternal hope in Jesus Christ.

We know people that have gone through infinitely harder things than us. Currently, Christians around the world are being killed for their belief in Christ and persecuted. I bet you those Christians are rejoicing as it's happening. We hear story after story after story of martyrs, and people who believe in Jesus rejoice because of the hope they have. As I said, this gospel is not just about having a happy and comfortable life now but having eternal hope in Jesus Christ; we will spend eternity with our heavenly father. This life is temporary, and there are going to be hard things. It won't always be easy, but we like it works for you.

## What fellowship does light have with darkness?

In 2 Corinthians 6:14, the question is raised: 'Don't become partners with those who do not believe, for what partnership is there between righteousness and lawlessness, or what fellowship does light have with darkness?' So, when we think about a yoke, agricultural terms an apparatus that is put around the neck of Ox and this scripture also refers to the Rotary 22 and 10 that talks about and that scripture was saying don't pair an ox to a donkey and when they were plowing their purpose is create nothing but straight lines in order to grow your crop the correct way.

## Working in the same direction.

If you are yoking two oxen together, it's important to ensure they are of the same size, weight, and strength to create a straight line while plowing. So when you think about this scripture, you feel about your life; the whole purpose is for us to grow and develop our marriage. If we want to walk a straight line and if we want our marriage to be fruitful, we want our marriage to grow. I don't want to be yoked with someone of unequal spirituality. If my partner believes in Christ, practices her belief, and loves Jesus as I do, we are walking in the same direction. The Bible talks about the relationship between light and darkness, as well as believers and unbelievers. The Bible also talks about bad company corrupting good character. As a parent, you don't want your kid to hang around with that lousy kid because you don't want that bad kid to rub off on your good kid. If that's the case in our friendships, why are we so loose about our marriages? I didn't know what yoke was; obviously didn't know how to spell yoke. I was still spelling it YOLK, but yeah, so I would meet these people, and naturally, once they realize I am a church girl, one of the things that they may say to impress me is that

## Going to church does not mean being a Christian.

They are Christian or that they go to church, and you know, for a person who's already going to church, you naturally think, oh wow, cool, you know he's a church guy. I could actually take him home to meet mom one day. As time went on, I realized that their talk didn't necessarily match their walk. I did not even grasp it until when I met this gentleman. His excitement got me excited, but to meet someone who not just believed but really wanted to study the word of God and more loser to God that made me feel like, hey, you know what this is? Who I need to be linked up with this is who I need to be yoked with. Not why OK with and because. It's important to yoke yourself with someone who is walking towards God if you want a godly marriage. That individual walking towards God, and you're walking towards. God you are going to end up meeting right there in the middle. Though it may not always be easy on this path, we've had our battles and tough times. We have our testimony however, at the end of the day, we are yoked with the right person, and we're able to come back together again and have this ministry where we can talk to you.

## To be married less will be called singleness more will be called to marriage, so marriage is right.

Does this mean that you can date and marry an unbeliever? That's what we're going to discuss in this episode. Hey everybody, there are things we have to do in a relationship. Even getting married is not a command; it's something that God has made. Christians to be married less will be called singleness more will be called to marriage, so marriage is absolutely right, but it's not a command. Your heart's desires play an important role in who you choose to marry or if you should marry at all. It's not like this, you know, rigid thing in the Bible. There are a lot of personal choices involved, but there are some limits that the scriptures put on Christ

## He must not divorce her.

Versus 12 through 16, and people feel like this passage is justification for why it's OK to marry a non-believer. So here's what this passage says. It says to the rest. I say this. I, not the Lord. If any brother has a wife who is not a believer and she is willing to live with him, he must not divorce her. If a woman has a husband who is not a believer. He is willing to live with her; she must not divorce him for the unbelieving husband has been sanctified through his life through his wife, and the unbelieving wife has been sanctified through her believing husband; otherwise, your children would be unclean and but as it is, they are holy but. However, if the non-believer chooses to leave, the believer is not bound in such circumstances. In all things, God has called us to live in peace.

## How do you know if you, as a wife, will save your husband, or how do you know if you, as a husband, will save your wife?

How do you know wife whether you will save your husband or how do you know husband whether you will save your wife. Paul is talking about a situation where an unbeliever is married to a believer. He is asking how you should approach divorce and this type of marriage. So a lot of people say the post talking about that it must be OK for Christians to marry non-Christians, but that is really taking this passage out of context. This passage is not condoning marrying an unbeliever it's condemning divorcing a spouse that you're already married to who's an unbeliever. In other words, there are times when two non-Christians get married, which is biblical.

## The Bible advises against divorcing an unequally yoked spouse. Once you make a covenant commitment with someone, God wants you to honor that commitment and avoid divorce.

At first, the couple is equally yoked, but then one of them comes to salvation through Jesus Christ while the other remains an unbeliever. The Bible says if that's your case, you should not just divorce because you're unequally yoked. Since you have already made a covenant marriage commitment to this person, God does not want you to divorce them unless the unbelieving spouse wants to leave the believing spouse. In that case, the Christian spouse is free to let the person go and get a divorce. However, Paul advises against it.

## Your example could potentially save your spouse.

This is literally saying, like you being in proximity in the marriage and remaining in the marriage, that your life could potentially, and your example could potentially save your spouse, so why don't you read those scriptures? I'm your set of scriptures. I'm going to start with first Peter three, one through 2, w says, likewise wives be subject to your own husband so that if some do not obey the word, they may be one without a word by the conduct of their wives when they see your respectful and pure conduct. So, this is a really powerful verse, and I just love that this verse is in here because it's just encouragement to the wife's heart; you know, earlier, we talked about endurance.

## Because you are practicing righteousness before your spouse.

And enduring the weight of having an unbelieving spouse, and there's power here in the way that we can conduct ourselves according to scripture according to God's word. Scripture calls for us to exhibit respectful and pure conduct, which means living out our beliefs with integrity and purity, particularly in our relationships with unbelieving spouses. And it says right here that they may be one without a word like you don't even need to go into explaining why you're doing the things that you're doing, although if they ask, I mean by all means, give them the answer because it's powerful but God saying it's your contact that's going to reveal it. Because the reality is you couldn't potentially you couldn't in reality

## I should say speak to your spouse 24/7 about what the word says enter and convince them to become a Christian that actions are so powerful.

Speak to your spouse 24/7 about what the word says and convince them to become a Christian that actions are so powerful. Still, they will see your actions every day, so again, if you say one thing and do another right; they will never believe you. They're not going to see it as they're not going to your life isn't going to betray the truth of what you say is true. But when you say things to them, you know the reason. I believe what the Bible says because 'You know what God's done in my life, and this is what I believe in Jesus. Then when I see you back that way, when they see you walk that way, they'll be like, whoa, you know I can't stop this. What's happening? Why does this person love me so much, especially when I treat them this way or when I don't believe what they believe or so. Even though this is specifically talking to the wives and in her role and the way she can walk out the gospel in her marriage to an unbelieving spouse or an or a spouse that's not obeying the word because we talked about in the beginning right so it could be an unbelieving spouse or it could be totally disobedient like that one husband at the beginning of our or you know this episode, but the principle can still work that.

## We treat our spouses the way the Bible tells us to treat them.

We treat our spouse the way the Bible tells us to treat them when we walk out of this Gospel, and it actually, later on in verse seven, says how a husband can treat his wife. If you want to read that for sure, it says, likewise, husbands live with their wives in an understanding way showing honor to the woman as the weaker vessel since they're heirs with you of the grace of life so that your prayers may not be hindered. So again, this is some people might think this verse is controversial but

**The husband recognizes, like Oh my gosh, I am going to walk with my wife in an understanding way. I am going to show her that I understand her. I am going to work to teach her and love her.**

I find it beautiful when a husband commits to walking with his wife in understanding, showing her love, and working on learning about her. This aligns with the Biblical command in Ephesians 5:25 for husbands to love their wives as Christ loves the church. If you look at the gospel, the husband represents Christ in the marriage and is sacrificial in his love for her and wash her still in the word. Even if she doesn't share his beliefs, he can still live out those biblical roles and commands as a Christian husband to an unbelieving wife. The husband can walk with his wife in understanding, recognizing that they both share in the grace of life. As discussed earlier, this requires a godly perspective as a commitment to supporting one’s spouse. And so you know even though Jennifer and

## We are supposed to look at the world; we do not look at it through just our own opinions or even through just our own experiences.

I have never personally experienced this, but we don't have to rely solely on our own opinions or experiences to understand the world. The word of God provides guidance on how we should view the world. Our personal experiences may be biased and lead us to think in ways that are not in line with biblical teachings. The Bible is unchanging and inherently provides a clear framework for understanding the world. And I think it's beautiful that God knew that we would need this guide on how to interact within a marriage where there's an unequally yoked relationship. Lastly, the most beautiful part about this is none of this has anything to do with just having a happy marriage, right? Like it's not just about, you know, being healthy and happy and joyful and like, 'oh as long if my husband got saved, you know things would be much better, which they would be, but we have hardships.

## Believers, you know, so the point is not just to have a comfortable, happy marriage, the point is to be holy, and the point is the salvation of your spouse's soul is the most important thing.

In our marriage, as believers, we understand that a comfortable and happy marriage is not the ultimate goal. The point is to be holy, and the point is this the salvation of your spouse's soul is the most important thing. This is why Christ came to the world. It is what God's doing in the world as he's through Christ reconciling people to himself that we would have eternity with him right so as we've given all this encouragement to a spouse who may be married to an unbeliever or someone who isn't walking that way what would you say to the person listening to us right now who is that spouse who's unbelieving or maybe isn't walking in obedience to God's word so.

## It's true that Jesus came to save us. He reconciles us with the father so we can have a great relationship with him. Without Jesus, we can't save ourselves.

First of all, I would say repent and believe in the Lord Jesus. It's true that Jesus came to save us and reconcile us with the father so we can have the right relationship with him. Without Jesus, we can't save ourselves. We need a savior to be renewed, regenerated, and filled with the Holy Spirit that he's promised us. The Holy Spirit will empower us to walk in freedom, strength, and authority.

## You should believe today that you love so much that they would share the gospel that they want you to be saved.

If you don't believe in Gospel that your loved ones share with you, you should still believe in the Lord Jesus. So that you would be in heaven with them one day that's our goal is that we want to be an eternity with our father in heaven and not eternal separation from him. That's the truth, that's the gospel, and it's a good gospel. It's called the good news and the reason for hope. I mean, I don't know how other people do it in this world without the saving knowledge of Christ because with it in our lives and the hardships that we've endured, there is hope, there's a future, and we are just we're excited about it. It fuels us. Yeah, and no matter what happens in this life, like I said, it's not just about comfortable, or you know, happily ever after; it's about eternal hope. Yeah because man

**Rejoice in persecution. People who believe in Jesus rejoice because of the hope they have and so, like I said, this gospel is not just that we would have a happy, comfortable life now, but that we have eternal hope in Jesus Christ.**

We know people that have gone through infinitely harder things than us. Currently, Christians around the world are being killed for their belief in Christ and persecuted. I bet you those Christians are rejoicing as it's happening. We hear story after story after story of martyrs, and people who believe in Jesus rejoice because of the hope they have. As I said, this gospel is not just about having a happy and comfortable life now but having eternal hope in Jesus Christ; we will spend eternity with our heavenly father. This life is temporary, and there are going to be hard things. It won't always be easy, but we like it works for you.

## What fellowship does light have with darkness?

In 2 Corinthians 6:14, the question is raised: 'Don't become partners with those who do not believe, for what partnership is there between righteousness and lawlessness, or what fellowship does light have with darkness?' So, when we think about a yoke, agricultural terms an apparatus that is put around the neck of Ox and this scripture also refers to the Rotary 22 and 10 that talks about and that scripture was saying don't pair an ox to a donkey and when they were plowing their purpose is create nothing but straight lines in order to grow your crop the correct way.

## Working in the same direction.

If you are yoking two oxen together, it's important to ensure they are of the same size, weight, and strength to create a straight line while plowing. So when you think about this scripture, you feel about your life; the whole purpose is for us to grow and develop our marriage. If we want to walk a straight line and if we want our marriage to be fruitful, we want our marriage to grow. I don't want to be yoked with someone of unequal spirituality. If my partner believes in Christ, practices her belief, and loves Jesus as I do, we are walking in the same direction. The Bible talks about the relationship between light and darkness, as well as believers and unbelievers. The Bible also talks about bad company corrupting good character. As a parent, you don't want your kid to hang around with that lousy kid because you don't want that bad kid to rub off on your good kid. If that's the case in our friendships, why are we so loose about our marriages? I didn't know what yoke was; obviously didn't know how to spell yoke. I was still spelling it YOLK, but yeah, so I would meet these people, and naturally, once they realize I am a church girl, one of the things that they may say to impress me is that

## Going to church does not mean being a Christian.

They are Christian or that they go to church, and you know, for a person who's already going to church, you naturally think, oh wow, cool, you know he's a church guy. I could actually take him home to meet mom one day. As time went on, I realized that their talk didn't necessarily match their walk. I did not even grasp it until when I met this gentleman. His excitement got me excited, but to meet someone who not just believed but really wanted to study the word of God and more loser to God that made me feel like, hey, you know what this is? Who I need to be linked up with this is who I need to be yoked with. Not why OK with and because. It's important to yoke yourself with someone who is walking towards God if you want a godly marriage. That individual walking towards God, and you're walking towards. God you are going to end up meeting right there in the middle. Though it may not always be easy on this path, we've had our battles and tough times. We have our testimony however, at the end of the day, we are yoked with the right person, and we're able to come back together again and have this ministry where we can talk to you.

## To be married less will be called singleness more will be called to marriage, so marriage is right.

Does this mean that you can date and marry an unbeliever? That's what we're going to discuss in this episode. Hey everybody, there are things we have to do in a relationship. Even getting married is not a command; it's something that God has made. Christians to be married less will be called singleness more will be called to marriage, so marriage is absolutely right, but it's not a command. Your heart's desires play an important role in who you choose to marry or if you should marry at all. It's not like this, you know, rigid thing in the Bible. There are a lot of personal choices involved, but there are some limits that the scriptures put on Christ

## How do you know if you, as a wife, will save your husband, or how do you know if you, as a husband, will save your wife?

How do you know wife whether you will save your husband or how do you know husband whether you will save your wife. Paul is talking about a situation where an unbeliever is married to a believer. He is asking how you should approach divorce and this type of marriage. So a lot of people say the post talking about that it must be OK for Christians to marry non-Christians, but that is really taking this passage out of context. This passage is not condoning marrying an unbeliever it's condemning divorcing a spouse that you're already married to who's an unbeliever. In other words, there are times when two non-Christians get married, which is biblical.

## The Bible advises against divorcing an unequally yoked spouse. Once you make a covenant commitment with someone, God wants you to honor that commitment and avoid divorce.

At first, the couple is equally yoked, but then one of them comes to salvation through Jesus Christ while the other remains an unbeliever. The Bible says if that's your case, you should not just divorce because you're unequally yoked. Since you have already made a covenant marriage commitment to this person, God does not want you to divorce them unless the unbelieving spouse wants to leave the believing spouse. In that case, the Christian spouse is free to let the person go and get a divorce. However, Paul advises against it.

## You need to stay married

If you're a Christian and your spouse is a non-christian who wants to stay with you, you do not have a biblical license to divorce that person. You need to stay married. This is not a passage about condoning marrying non-believer. It's a passage forbidding divorcing a non-believing spouse. This was also very prevalent in Paul's day because we have to remember Christianity was just starting at this point. So obviously, there were tons of people coming to faith who were married to people who were coming to faith. These people didn't know Christianity at that time, so they were all unbelievers.

## Paul is giving advice on how to handle that

There were some who were coming to faith. There's going to be a high population of mismatches in marriages between believers and non-believers. Paul is giving advice on how to handle that. It does not mean that this was now a reason you could marry a non-believer. That's because that scripture never contradicts scripture. Whenever you have a passage in the Bible that you're not sure about, or maybe it's a little bit confusing to you, what you want to do is you want to go to a part of the Bible that you are sure about, you want to go and see something that is extremely clear in scripture so that you can use one piece of scripture to interpret another piece of scripture. That's how you know the fancy word "hermeneutics." If you ever go to seminary or really get into theology, "hermeneutics" is the study of scripture and the interpretation of scripture. How do you do that? One principle in Hermeneutics is that scripture interprets scripture.

## The Bible will never contradict itself

If you're ever confused about something, you want to go to a passage that you're not confused about because the Bible will never contradict itself. You have to take the clear passage of scripture and interpret the unclear passage of scripture that you're confused about through what you do know. So, I think that passage that we just read is very clear, but if you're confused about it, let me just read you one more verse from the same chapter, first Corinthians Chapter 7, verse 39; here's what it says, "a woman is bound to her husband as long as he lives, but if her husband dies she is free to marry anyone she wishes, but he must belong to the Lord." I don't think it can get any clearer than that in first Corinthians 7 verse 39; it says that OK if your husband dies, or you know this applies to husbands as well, if your wife dies, you're free to marry someone.

## I do not know how you get around that passage and say, "Well, I can marry a non-Christian"

The only thing that Paul says here is that they have to belong to the Lord, so I don't know how you get around that passage and say, "Well, I can marry a non-Christian." That person does not belong to the Lord like a Christian does, so you know, first Corinthians 7 39 clearly says, "You must marry a Christian, so I don't know how verses

16 through or 12 through 16 would say that yeah it's OK for you to marry a non-Christian. The Bible never contradicts itself, so I think it's really clear that Paul was obviously talking about two different things. One, don't divorce someone if you already are married to them, and they want to stay with you, and then if you're unmarried, do not marry a non-christian.

## You are going to want to resolve in your heart to put God first no matter what you do

You're going to want to resolve in your heart to put God first no matter what you do. You have to make sure that you've settled it in your heart that you're not going to choose a relationship over Jesus Christ. That's step one. Within that idea, I believe it's wise and really important that you also settle in your heart what you believe the Bible actually says about dating a non-believer and marrying a non-believer. I'm not going to go into that topic in depth in this video because I've done that multiple times on other videos which. I can leave a link to that playlist in the description of this video but. In short, I believe the Bible is extremely clear that Christians are not supposed to marry non-believers. It clearly expresses that in First Corinthians 7 verse 39 and also in multiple other places like Second Corinthian 6 where it says, "do not be unequally yoked with an unbeliever."

## I also believe dating a non-believer is unbiblical

Because of that verse, I also believe dating a non-believer is unbiblical. You're being yoked together through dating even though it's not as big of a bond as Christian marriage. However, I believe that's something that God forbids. Some people don't believe that about the dating side, and some people don't even believe that about the marriage side. Again, I've studied it. I feel like it's pretty clear, but whatever you decide, you have to make sure your answer is firmly rooted in scripture and not just something that you're making up on your own. The second step I would encourage you to take is to commit to not missionary date this person. Missionary Dating is a term that many Christians use where they're using a relationship as a way of being a light to a non-believer, and so they say, "Well, I really like this person, they don't know Jesus, aren't Christians supposed to be a light to the world, if they don't know Christ." Yes, they are, but again, we can't contradict other parts of scripture, like being unequally yoked. I have a whole other video in that playlist I mentioned, and it's all about missionary dating. In essence, the big reason I don't believe in missionary dating is that, one, you're unequally yoked, but number two; it's a really terrible foundation to start a relationship on. Trying to change someone. You're not just getting into a relationship because you really like them and you want to grow together, but you're specifically trying to change them. You're saying I don't like the way you are. I want you to change, and I'm going to use this relationship to change who you are, and that's just really not a foundation for a healthy relationship. If you're a Christian, you should be joined by another Christian, and you want to help each other grow and build each other up,

## Live in a Biblical relationship

You shouldn't look at someone and say, "Wow! I like you, but I want you to totally change who you are, and therefore, I'm going to try to manipulate everything to make you into someone I want you to be, even though you're not that person right now." Again, that's manipulative. It's not a good foundation to build up, and I believe just being in that relationship, in general, is unbiblical .3 is to assume in your heart that this relationship is not going to work out romantically and that this person is not the one. The reason I say that is because you should start there, and you should assume that this person is not going to become a Christian one day.

## Like the way you can guard your heart when you are doing these other things

I think it's OK to be open to the idea, maybe, to even say, "Man! I wish that would happen. I really like this person, and they have great qualities." To be open to that idea if it happened? Sure, go for it but to actually assume that it will happen and arrange your life around this thing that's not reality and is very unlikely to become a reality. It is extremely unwise, and it's not going to help you guard your heart as you interact with this person like the way you can guard your heart when you're doing these other things. So all this to say, like the ways that you can witness to this person I don't think you should do that just.

## You should be a witness to this person who does not know Christ

You really want to date them. I think you should be a witness to this person who doesn't know Christ because we're supposed to be a witness to the lost world and help people who don't know Jesus Christ. That's fine to do. That's good to do, but assuming that it's not going to work and assuming that this isn't the person God has for you is wise. Again, for a few reasons. Because it's probably not like you're going to marry one person. You're going to meet thousands of people that you could marry, but you're not going to marry. So again, statistically, it's just a good assumption to make. Secondly, as you're interacting, as you're maybe building a friendship or inviting this person to your Christian community, having that assumption in your heart will help you guard your heart and not go down a road that you shouldn't be going down with a non-believer.

## Way to guard your heart; The fourth thing that you can do when you have feelings for this person.

Now let's say, "Hey, it all works out." Your assumption was wrong. This person really becomes a Christian and loves God. They're growing. They become your husband or wife one day. You could be pleasantly surprised; your assumption doesn't mean that it can never happen, but, again, it's just a good way to guard your heart. It is the fourth thing that you can do when you have feelings for this person by not dating them so you can actually show this person the love of Christ and show this person what it means to be a follower of Christ; by obeying God's word even when it's difficult. So to me, another reason missionary dating is a bad idea is that it just seems totally contradictory.

## God's word by becoming unequally yoked and not obeying God, hoping that this person one day obeys God

You're saying I want this person to become a Christian and obey God's word, and to do that, I'm going to contradict God's word by becoming "unequally yoked" and not obeying God, hoping that this person one day obeys God because I'm a witness to them?" You see how that, to me, doesn't really make sense. By not dating this person, by putting Jesus Christ above this relationship, you're actually going to be a light to this person. In the process, you're not going to have the relationship you want, but that says a lot to someone who isn't following Jesus. When they see that you're willing to sacrifice for God, that you're willing to do hard things when they probably know that you like them, but you're not going to date them because it goes against your beliefs and your passion for God, that's going to be a huge witness to that person. It's one of the best ways that you can be a light to this person that you have feelings for.

## The way that you go about interacting with the world will figure out if you are going to get pulled down or pulled up.

The 5th step that you can take when you have feelings for a non-believer is to witness them by bringing them into your Christian community rather than joining them in their non-Christian community. The way that you go about interacting with the world will determine if you're going to get pulled down or whether you're going to help non- believers get pulled up. It's extremely easy to have good intentions but to get so close to evil and worldliness and things that you know are non-Christian is getting dragged down yourself. One helpful way is to be a witness to a non-believer, not to isolate yourself and surround yourself with a lot of people who don't know God as a way of witnessing; rather, if you are building a relationship with a non-Christian friend, it's wiser to take that person out of their secular non-Christian community and bring them into your Christian community where that person can see other Christians besides just you. It's also really helpful because if this person really is going to become a Christian and they're going to start maturing in the Lord, they're going to need people of the same gender to help them grow.

## Do not get pulled down like that

You can't be their main discipleship partner if you guys have feelings for each other. You're of the opposite gender. This person needs a community of Christians if they're actually going to become a Christian. So those are a few reasons. It's really wise to be strategic and don't just go to the bar or go to the club or go to the non-Christian party under the assumption of, "Hey, I'm going to be a light for the world." That's unwise, and you're going to get pulled down like that.

## Brothers! If anyone is caught in any transgression, you who are spiritual should restore him in a spirit of gentleness

It says for example, Galatians 6 verse one says, "brothers, if anyone is caught in any transgression, you who are spiritual should restore him in a spirit of gentleness but keep watch on yourself lest you too be tempted." So right there, Paul says, "yes, go and try to help people who are stuck in the world but be careful that you are not also pulled down by the temptations." that they are struggling with or, for example

## It says in First Corinthians 15:33 says, "do not be deceived; bad company ruins good morals"

It says in First Corinthians 15:33, "Do not be deceived; bad company ruins good morals." A good character, as it says in the NIV translation, "Just be wise, and one way that you can be wise is by using your Christian community to also be a light to this person. The 6th way that you can help this person that you like who is a non-believer is to serve them in friendship, in Group settings, so just as I talked about the importance of a Christian community.

## Guarding your heart well

A group setting is going to help you out a lot because if you have feelings for someone, then you're spending a lot of one-on-one on one time with that person. You're going to like that person more, and you're not going to be guarding your heart well. If you're always spending one-on- one time with this person, basically saying that you're just friends but acting like boyfriend and girlfriend, but you just don't want the title, that's really unwise. You're going to progress down that line of having more and more feelings for this person, which, again, is something you want to avoid. You want to serve this person and be a light to this person, but you don't want to be so tempted and start liking this person more and more.

## You are going to, you know, start dating them and turn your back on God for this relationship

You're going to actually start dating them and turn your back on God for this relationship. The 7th step that you should take when you have feelings for an unbeliever and you're trying to be a witness to this person is to be honest about your feelings, and if you're getting pulled down and you like this person more and more, you're going to need to put up bigger boundaries. All the things that I've talked about so far, I think, are helpful and wise, but you also have to be honest about your ability to maintain your emotions and not get sucked into a relationship that God is leading you not to have. If you're not being honest and you just let yourself go, it's going to end badly. You have to be honest and say, "Am I spiritually mature enough? Am I relationally mature enough? Do I like this person too much? Are my feelings just out of control?"

## If they become a Christian, they start bearing the fruits of the spirit

If you're saying yes to those questions, then you need to take a step back and put up bigger boundaries and realize this is not working. What I'm trying to do is that I need to be careful and put my walk with

God. But if they ever become a Christian and they start bearing the fruits of the spirit, then you should be open to getting into a relationship with this person. Again, that's a lot of steps that need to happen before. I would recommend being open to being in a relationship with this person, but I don't think you would be wrong if a non-believer genuinely became a Christian and they weren't just saying they were a Christian so that you two could date. They really put their faith in Jesus Christ. They really repented of their sins, and then most importantly, they were actually displaying the fruits of the spirit, and they were actually showing that not only are they professing with their mouth that Jesus is Lord but that the way they live their life is evidence of the salvation they received.

## There is something with you that I hope could encourage you a little bit

Then only I think there's something with you that I hope could possibly encourage you a little bit, and that is that I'm sorry to hear about the situation that your marriage is in. As your brother in Christ, I mourn with you even the loss of the dream so far of a marriage between two people that love each other and two people that are to love God and one another. I'm sorry for that, for I have experienced this pain first-hand that you are experiencing. I myself was in that marriage for nearly 15 years.

## God helped me to see much relief

We had many weak moments in my story, but we somehow seemed to continue to be able to move forward, and really what it was

was just that for the sake of peace. We swept things under the rug. That's really the truth, and then the issue was always there, and eventually, that route would begin to produce more .fruit. We were never getting to the cause. I just want to share something with you. There's a principle that God helped me to see much relief. I'm not saying that this necessarily applies to your situation because I don't know what the father would do in your situation, but it is something that happened to me.

## Christians believe that divorce is not something that you should do

It does happen often, and that is obvious. I did not want to end my marriage. I wanted to be one of those who were married, 90 years old, walking down the beach hand in hand with my wife as lovers. That was a dream that I had, and because I was a Christian man, I did not want to divorce my wife. I think I put up with, as most people would say, I went far beyond what most people would have to accommodate. My Christian beliefs are that divorce is not something that you should do. There are three instances that the Bible gives for the separation of marriage.

## When it not sinful to be divorced

The first one is that of Matthew chapter 5. It talks about marital unfaithfulness as the only reason that a man can divorce his wife. There are also two other instances where a marriage can be broken, where in the eyes of God, it is not considered evil or adultery, or sinful, and that is through the death of one spouse if somebody becomes a widow. Another option can be found in First Corinthians 7:15, where we see that sometimes an unbelieving spouse will leave the marriage because of the other person's belief in Jesus Christ. Paul teaches that the believing spouse should let the unbelieving spouse leave in that manner and that you, the believing spouse, are no longer bound in that marriage.

## Yet realize the difference between a false disciple and a true disciple

The reason Paul gives is that God desires that we live in peace. This is first Corinthians Chapter 7, verse 15. Now, how you define a "non-believer" was interesting to me because I did not yet realize the difference between a false disciple and a true disciple. I did not really understand the difference at this time between knowing about God versus knowing God, and there was a great deal of time that would pass before I began to understand these principles of God. I do want to share with you something that happened. There was a man who came into my life and tried to counsel my eye. He's a famous man, and he came into our life. He had a situation where his marriage was saved at the last minute. Now they were both Christians, and they had completely gone through the divorce process.

They were within days of signing the papers when somebody asked them to make a last-ditch effort and go to this marriage treat in Arkansas.

## Miraculously God saved their marriage

So they went, and miraculously God saved their marriage. A friend of mine knew this man, and he and my friend knew that my wife and I were very much in dire straits and were trying our last-ditch efforts to save the marriage. He set up a meeting together with my wife and me and this other man and his wife. We went to meet them, and they bring their divorce papers to show us that they were all done except for the sign and that God can do these amazing miracles. I so badly wanted to believe. When we leave the meeting, I feel a sense of hope, but soon after, things just get worse, and as you have seen in my story I'm I think you've seen my story I'm not sure.

A wife would go through the process of separating from me and she would even file for divorce within two weeks of separating. Well as it turns out, I was in a leadership group and I drove out to the middle of nowhere for a leadership conference., and gues who is the speaker? It's this man Jeff who spoke to my wife and I with his wife. He's the speaker and I'm embarrassed because they tried to help us save the marriage and it hasn't been saved, it's gotten worse. So I went up to him and I said, “Hey!” and he said, “Mike, how's it going? How.”

You know what? I said, “Jeff I'm so sorry to tell you this man, I don't even know how to explain to you.”I said, “It's gotten so bad, it's like spiritual warfare on a level I've never seen. She not only separated but she has now filed for divorce and then she has just turned into like a monster! It's unbelievable. I just, I'm embarrassed and humiliated to tell you and and it's just, you know, but I'm just trusting God.”

These are the words that come out of his mouth. He says to me something that just rocked my world, because in the church, all we hear about is how much God hates divorce. “God hates divorce, if you get divorced you have scarlet letter A on your chest, or scarlet D. It should be but you know and you feel so much pressure and you can feel such a loss and such complete failure. That’s not useful to God, you know, it's humiliating and it rips your

## In times of trouble, a Leader, pastor, Doctor, or marriage counselor is important.

A wife would go through the process of separating from me, and she would even file for divorce within two weeks of separating well; as it turns out, I was in a leadership group, and I drove out to the middle of nowhere for a leadership conference, and who is the speaker it's this man Jeff who spoke to my wife and me with his wife he's the speaker and I'm embarrassed because here they tried to help us save the marriage and it hasn't been saved it's gotten worse so I went up to him, and I said Jeff I said hey he said Mike how's it going how you know what I said Jeff I'm so sorry to tell you this man I said I don't even know how to explain to you I said it's gotten so bad.

## God hates divorce.

I said it's like spiritual warfare on a level I've never seen. I said she not only separated, but she's also now filed for divorce, and then she's just turned into like a monster. It's unbelievable. I am I'm embarrassed and humiliated to tell you, and it's just, you know, but I'm just trusting God. These are the words that come out of his mouth Christina he says to me something that just rocked my world because in church, all we hear about is how much God hates divorce. If you get divorced, you have a scarlet letter A on your chest, you know, or scarlet D it should be, but you know, and you feel so much pressure, and you can feel like such a loss and such a complete failure no useful to God you know it humiliating, and it rips your heart out I've been

## Let man not separate what God has joined together

It's hard getting in the way of what God wants to do. We shouldn't be surprised when he removes the other spouse. When he said that to me, Christina, it just was like I found freedom. I found, oh are you whoa. It was very hard for me to come to grips with it because the church only ever taught that divorce is bad. Another thing that I'm going to share with you is that God opened my eyes to thatHe gave me such relief. One day I was walking in the woods, and I was praying, and I said, "God, you know the Bible says "let man not separate what God has joined together. " I said, "I feel so bad." One day, I was just walking and praying, and it was like God said to me, "I didn't put this marriage together; you did, Christina." It was unbelievable. This spirit of God set me free and helped me see. When I met my wife, I was 19 years old, and the spirit of God just helped me to see that I was the one that put this marriage together, not him.

## I endured suffering and bore some of the extra sufferings of Christ in my body

If he had not ended the marriage like he did and had not used my ex-wife in such a brutal way in my life, I would not be the person I am today. I would not be enjoying this amazing relationship with my father in heaven. That is beyond putting into words. With what I have today, I can walk through the valley of the shadow of death. I endured suffering II bore some of the extra sufferings of Christ in my body, and God has helped me so much. So, I just want to encourage you that no matter what happens, as long as you continue to position yourself to seek God and you obey him. You act Christ-like, let your husband do whatever he needs to do.

## God is saying to you let go of what is dead

It very well may be that revival breaks out in your heart and in your life, and he separates from you because that is exactly what happened to me, if that is God's will. Now, it could also be that it's God's will to save him radically at the last minute. I don't want to give you false hope, but that is possible; that is what God could do. He could do anything. My brotherly advice to you as my sister in Christ would be to hold this very loosely. Don't try to manipulate, don't try to save and hold on to that which is dead. It very well could be that God is saying to you, "Let go of what is dead in the past, and I will give you what is new in the future." Sometimes it is easier to give birth than it is to raise the dead and contrary to what you'll hear in the church. Sometimes revival comes from separation. The church preaches unity, but there are many stories throughout history where

God has used separation from people and separation in marriage and relationships to bring about revival. Remember Matthew 10;34, Jesus says, "Do not suppose that I have come to bring peace but a sword. I did not come to bring peace to the earth."

## You cannot love your loved ones (Father, Mother, Wife and children, Brother, and sister) more than God

He says, "I have come to divide the son against father, to divide mother from daughter daughter-in-law from mother-in-law; a man's enemies will be the members of his own household, anyone who loves father or mother more than me is not worthy of me, anyone who loves his brother or sister more than me is not worthy of me, and anyone who does not take up his cross and follow after me is not worthy of me." Understand God's top priority Christina; if you are seeking God, his top priority is your heart. His top priority is to conform you to the image of Christ Jesus (Romans 8:29).

Why? It's his glory that's at stake. God is about his glory. In your life, God works through us, in us, and for us, ultimately for him. So, if anybody wants to get in the way of what God wants to glorify himself in their life, that person is robbing God of his glory. There is nothing on this earth, no relationship, no marriage, no child, no finances, no career, no mission; nothing is as important on this earth as God's glory to himself.

## God wants to use you and move in you to bring glory to himself

If God wants to use you and move in you to bring glory to himself, and your ex-husband has remained hard-hearted, he has remained obstinate, and he has remained with his heels in the ground, you would not be surprised that God himself will remove him out of your life. It doesn't mean it won't be painful, but it is a good thing if God does it. So, I beg of you to hold it loosely. Don't do anything to manipulate or accelerate this. Let it be that if he is to be run off that God runs him off. You must continue to be a woman of noble character. You must continue to hold your head high, and you must continue to pray for him as he is currently your enemy because Jesus Christ said, “He who is not with me is against me.”

## Above all things, guard your heart

He who does not gather scatters, that means that your husband is living as an enemy of the cross, of Christ. You have an enemy of your master in your household. You must understand that is exactly how God sees it. This is why Paul warns us not to be unequally yoked with those of unbelievers because their sinful nature is enmity towards God. It despises God, and it cannot follow God's law. Romans age seven so. I just pray, dear sister, that you will consider all this. I hope this is something for you to be encouraged by, and I know no matter what, it's not fun to go through this. It's painful, it's brutal, but God will be with you. Christina, above all things, guard your heart for out of it flows the wellspring of life (Proverbs 4: 23). Guard your heart. Don't allow whatever the devil may want to do. If your husband leaves you, don't allow whatever kind of dirt he wants to throw at you to stain your heart.

## God's vengeance is overcoming evil not by being overcome by evil but by overcoming evil with good. Be Christ-like and be willing to suffer

You maintain a Christ-like position. Do not resist an evil person but turn the other cheek (Matthew 5: 39). Leave room for God's vengeance and overcome evil by not being overcome by evil but overcoming evil with good. Be Christ-like and be willing to suffer. Be willing to be wronged. You never can tell what kind of an impact that may have on his life. Be willing to let him have the other hand, be willing to let him take advantage of you. First Corinthians chapter 6. Go read that. Be willing to be wronged and be willing to be cheated.

## Just know you have a brother in Christ who is praying for you

Be willing to be thrown upon the mercy of God, where you have nothing but him, and you will find that when all you have is God, He is all you've ever needed, Christina. He is your father, and He loves you, and He can do amazing things in your life. I have many more things I could share with you, but for now, hopefully, this message will help you. Just know you have a brother in Christ who's praying for you, and I promise you, if you'll get in that book and you'll start actively putting the teachings of Christ into practice, he will blow your mind with his love for you. God bless. This book is very interesting.

## God's word is remarkably interesting. We have so much to say about this subject; An unbeliever with a believer is a big responsibility

God's word is very interesting. We have so much to say about this subject; an unbeliever with a believer is a big responsibility. There's one thing I want to say about my word that is when you question a situation like that, you're not asking anything bad to happen to your spouse, but the one thing I'm asking when that situation happens; ask Jesus for his grace because we are human, everybody, all humans. It says that there should be even one person that is home and says everyone has committed sin in their life. Like it says in John 360. God so loved the world that He sent Jesus to give salvation to whoever believed in him. That means there would be no salvation without Jesus.

## As the Bible says that the unbeliever is free to live, and so it is not a problem for that person to remarry because if the person marries and leave

I want to use it as my own word that in any situation, there is no other way that the unbeliever wants to go. As the Bible says, the unbeliever is free to live. It's not a problem for that person to remarry because if the person marries and leaves with pen and anxiety about his salvation. God sent Jesus to save those people because Jesus said that he didn't come to the world for those already healthy, those already like Moses, those already like Joshua, and those already like Isaiah. Jesus didn't come for those people but for those who really needed him. When I say we didn't need him, there would be no other way for those people to go to heaven because some people did not question, but they lived. They asked questions sometimes. I'm not going to say it's better, but they have good behavior. They follow the rules, and they respect the law because that there wasn't why we have the fallacies of so many other people that didn't want to believe in Jesus because they thought they did everything good enough that they didn't need Jesus.

## I want people to understand everyone needs Jesus

I'm saying something that I want people to understand everyone needs Jesus. Either you're good, either you're bad, either you are the best, you are always going to need Jesus. The reason why you're always going to need Jesus is because Jesus is the way. We're just not the way, but Jesus is. The winner ship with your spouse is not the way, but Jesus is the way because the problem that exists in the marriage cannot be the way for Jesus. I'm not going to encourage people to live with problems in their marriage because that isn't why we want to make sure we give you all the verses that can help you protect your marriage.

## Believe in Jesus; he is the only one who is going to wash away your sins

That can help you get the best marriage, and that can help you resolve any type of issue, any type of wobbling in your marriage. But let me tell you the only thing you can do. The only thing you can do is believe in Jesus. He is the only one who is going to wash away your sin. and they sent Jesus to forgive or not. They send not only in the past but in the past and the present, and future every other sin because the problem in the marriage is not the only problem that someone can have.

## Believing in Jesus is the only way you are going to wash away your sins

It's not the only sin that cannot happen in someone's life. God knows everything. Make sure you're not doing certain things according to yourself and say, "God is going to forgive me," but do everything possible. But we are humans. That is why Jesus came. Jesus is God. He said in the first Quentin, I think, verses 30, 35. I don't remember the chapter; I might put it later. He's not going to let us bear or carry a burden that is too heavy for us. That's what the Bible explains about the situation. Sometimes Jesus takes away the burden for you, and you think the burden is on your shoulder. The way the burden for you, but you take it on your shoulder When God already remove it for you

## True Christian, a true believer; You love God, you accepted Jesus in your life

This is what it says in this chapter. I think this testimony is a very interesting one because some situations are easier than others because that situation is a true question. When you are a true question, a true believer, you love God, you accept Jesus in your life, and you get to a point where you cannot do anything else. In verse, it says that division sometimes got used for his own glory. When I say some churches are divided, it is painful for some of them. They didn't feel good to see some of them go but knew that division made them stronger. People come to Jesus. They do more for the Kingdom of God because you had only one church. It divided into two. Now you have two churches. We're not going to encourage the vision, but at the same time, sometimes the vision happens for the glory of God. This is what I mean by what we need when we end the situation very difficult that we don't know what to do. We feel like we under God's law we fall down under God's law, but let me tell you, God knows everything.

## There is grace in Jesus's name

Suppose you don't have anything to protect yourself because you live with someone else, and that person doesn't care. Maybe that person is an unbeliever or someone that already lived the faith. That is not a question anymore, maybe, but how much do you need to do in a situation like that? Now you're going to see that you fall under God's law, but if you fall under God's law, what's going to happen? There is "grace." This is what I want to say today. There is grace in Jesus's name because there is only one way to heaven. That is through Jesus Christ. If you really believe in Jesus Christ, there is a way because God says in the Bible, "bound on the earth is also bound in the heaven." That is the reason why we have church leaders. There are certain situations you live in, and leaders must understand that according to the way it is.

## They do everything possible to solve the situation. If it is something that cannot be solved, then God knows everything. We are not going to be the ones that tell God what to do

They're not going to set standards according to their own perspective only, but they want to make sure they do everything possible to solve the situation. If it's something that cannot be solved, then God knows everything. We're not going to be the ones that tell God what to do. God already knows, and the other word she said in the testimony is very strong. She said in the testimony that God talked to her about a vision because when you pray, you are searching for God. You have a certain problem? God is going to talk to you. God tell her God did God tell him that God didn't choose that wife for him? You take. It's not. What God chooses for you is going to stay. Maybe you didn't play enough when you had to choose someone. Maybe you didn't choose someone with your own eyes, you didn't pray, and now you're paying the consequences, but even if you're paying the consequences, that doesn't mean that God is not going to do anything for you. It doesn't mean that God's not going to take care of you because something happened.

## Basically, what he is saying here is that I am giving you a new fresh command from God

“Hey, brother Alan what do I do if I'm a believer? I love Jesus, but my spouse does not.”

Once again, I'm going to share with you exactly what the Bible has to say about this, and then we're going to get into some very practical things that you need to do. Let's head over to First Corinthians, chapter 7, where Paul addresses three primary scenarios as it relates to marriage. Scenario number one is the ideal situation which is "a believer is married to another believer." Now notice what Paul says here about the situation. Here in verses 10 and 11, he says to the married people, "I give this command, not I but the Lord." Now, let's stop right there. Many people will say, "See, that's the reason why we don't need to listen to Paul because Paul himself says that this is my command, not the Lord, but what he's basically saying here is that I am giving you a new fresh command from God, a new revelation from God that Jesus Christ has not previously given."

## He is simply saying I am giving you something that Jesus has not previously mentioned

He does not deny his own authority in terms of giving the scripture. He's simply saying, "I'm giving you something that Jesus has not previously mentioned." Let's keep reading. It says here, "A wife must not separate from her husband, but if she does, she must remain unmarried or else be reconciled to her husband, and a husband must not divorce his wife." Paul makes it very clear here that the ideal situation is for a believer to stay married to another believer, but if, for whatever reason, that does not happen and one believer chooses to leave the other believer. Basically, Paul says you got two choices. A; you can either remain unmarried for the rest of your life, or B; you need to be reconciled to your original spouse. To make it very clear, Paul says the ideal situation is for you to either stay married or be remarried to your original spouse.

## He is simply saying I am giving you something that Jesus has not previously mentioned

Now, the second scenario is not ideal; this is when a believer is married to an unbeliever, and the unbeliever wants to stay married to the believing spouse. Now, we all have some things that he wants to say here about this, but before we get into this passage of scripture, it is very important for us to understand the cultural background of the book of first Corinthians, specifically Chapter 7. Essentially this was written to a lot of younger baby carnal Christians. A lot of them were Gentile Christians, who did not know God, and so many of them were using their newfound faith in Christ as an excuse to get divorced. They were saying, "Hey, it can't be God's will for me." A new believer and lover of Christ to be married to my Pagan spouse, so God must want me to divorce them. Paul says, "No, let me explain to you what you really need to do." Beginning in verse 12, it says here, "to the rest I say this, I, not the Lord, if any brother has a wife who is not a believer and she is willing, must not divorce her and if a woman has a husband who is not a believer and he is willing to live with her she must not divorce him."

## Otherwise, your children would be unclean, but as it is, they are holy

Paul makes it very clear here that if you are a believer and you're married to a non-believer, and that non-believer basically says, "Hey, I get it. You love Jesus, and I don't, but I still love you, and I want to be married to you." Paul says you have no biblical grounds or basis for divorcing that person. Now, the second thing that Paul says about a believer who's married to a non-believer and that non-believer wants to stay married to the believer is found in this next verse. It says, "For the unbelieving husband has been sanctified through his wife and the unbelieving wife has been sanctified through her believing husband; otherwise your children would be unclean, but as it is, they are holy."

This phrase requires a little bit of interpretation. Hold on now, stay with me because I'm getting to the practical things you need to do if you find yourself in a situation. I got to lay the foundation so many people will read this passage and say, "Well, wait a second, what does Paul mean when he says that the unbelieving spouse is sanctified through the believing spouse or your children are holy?"

## The word "sanctified" means set apart, and the word "holy" means set apart

Well, it certainly doesn't mean that your unbelieving spouse is safe because you are safe, but rather the word "sanctified" means "set apart," and the word "holy" means set apart. Essentially what Paul is saying is that any blessings that come from God to you because you are a believer, you are adopted by God, you are a child of God, anytime God blesses you, everyone else in your household is going to benefit from those blessings in such a way where they will also be in some ways, set apart because you are in that home. Essentially, whatever God does for you, everyone else in your home will benefit from it.

## If the unbeliever leaves, let it be so the brother or the sister is not bound in such circumstances. God has called us to live in peace

Now the third scenario is if a believer is married to a non-believer, but that non-believer now wants out of that marriage. This is what Paul says, "But if the unbeliever leaves, let it be, so the brother or the sister is not bound in such circumstances. God has called us to live in peace." How do you know wife, whether you will save your husband, or how do you know husband, whether you will save your wife? Paul makes it very clear. He says, "Hey, you may love your spouse, but if they don't love Jesus and they say I want out of this marriage, let them go." The reasoning behind it is, "Hey, you don't know whether they're going to be saved or not, and so because you don't know that, the Bible says you are not bound in such circumstances."

## Most scholars will interpret that and say, "That means that you are now free to marry someone else if they are a believer."

Now some people would interpret that differently, but most scholars will interpret that and say that means that you are now free to marry someone else as long as they are a believer. Now that we're crystal clear on exactly what the Bible teaches about each scenario, I want to zoom in on scenario #2, which is where the believer is married to a non-believer. The non-believer does not want out of that marriage. Basically, you and the believing spouse are stuck in that relationship. I've got seven pieces of advice/tips that I want to give you.

## Many times, people will have this newfound relationship with Christ, and they will neglect their responsibilities to their spouse

**Tip #1: "Don't have an affair with Jesus."**

I know that it sounds weird; to put Jesus and the word affair in the same sentence. Let me explain what I mean by that. Many times people will have this newfound relationship with Christ, and they will neglect their responsibilities to their spouse, and so now, Jesus gets all of their love, all of their affection, and all of their attention. They completely deny their spouse, and they deny all of their marital responsibilities and duties, like taking care of their spouse, because they say, "Hey, you know what? You don't love Jesus, Jesus loves me, and so Jesus is going to get all of my love." That is not what God wants you to do. He still wants you to maintain the same type of love, the same fervor, and the same servant spirit that you had, even though they are not a Christian.

## Against your morality, that goes against your integrity, that goes against some of the things that you believe as a Christian. Remember, the order of submission is always God first.

**Tip #2: "Do not compromise your relationship with Christ because of your relationship with your spouse."**

Now what I mean by this is oftentimes, if you're married to somebody who's not a believer, they may ask you to do certain things that go against your morality, that go against your integrity, and that go against some of the things that you believe as a Christian.

Remember, the order of submission is always God first and then family second. So, if you are ever feeling compromised in your integrity, you are under no obligation to submit to the demands or the desires of your unbelieving spouse.

## Never give up on the power of prayer if you are married to an unbeliever

**Tip #3: It goes without saying; Pray for them.**

I'm not talking about some basics. I'm talking about effectual, fervent, ongoing prayer. Years ago, I went to preach at a church on the subject of prayer. Interestingly enough, at the end of that surface, I had this old lady came up to me and said, "Brother Alan, I really loved your message, and it really struck me because I was praying for my husband for 20 years every single day that he would get saved and one day he came to know the Lord," and that just let me know that we should never give up on the power of prayer. So, if you are married to an unbeliever, there should not be a day that goes by that you do not seek the Lord and ask God to change their heart and soften their heart so they can come to a saving relationship with Christ.

## Whenever you are being mistreated by your spouse, you want to respond in such a way that your spouse is left saying, "Wow! the way I treated her the way that I treated him deserves this type of response

**Tip #4: Model a Christ-like behavior**

This is huge. First Peter, chapter 3, verse one, speaking to wives, but it also applies to men as well; it says here, "Wives, in the same way, submit yourselves to your own husbands so that if any of them do not believe the word, they may be won over without words, by the behavior of their wives when they see the purity and reverence of your lives."

So what you want to happen is that whenever you are being mistreated by your spouse, you want to respond in such a way that your spouse is left saying, "Wow! The way I treated her or the way that I treated him deserved this type of response, but wow, this person, my spouse, treated me in such a way that I didn't deserve. They treated me in a better way than I would have expected. How can I be more like that? How can I treat them the way they are treating me?" Ultimately, as you are modeling a Christ-like character, you are showing them what it really means to be a Christian in hopes that they will seek the same thing that you have.

## The more we may be pushing them away and not allowing God to do the work in their life

**Tip #5: Respect their unbelief.**

Now, what I mean here is this; oftentimes, whenever we come to saving our relationship with Christ and our spouse is not, we try to force our faith on our spouse because we're so excited about it, and we're like, "you just have to get this just like I do." I mean, Jesus would change your life. What we don't realize is that the more we are trying to force our faith on them, the more we may be pushing them away and not allowing God to do the work in their life. You want to be prepared to answer their questions. You want to invite them to church from time to time and invite them to the things that you think are going to help them grow spiritually, but whatever you do, do not try to force your belief on them because their hearts are not yet ripe and not yet softened to the truth.

## What I have seen repeatedly is that when the husband is not a believer, the woman tends to stunt her spiritual role because she follows or gives in to his leadership

**Tip #6: Continue to grow in your relationship with Jesus Christ now.**

I want to talk specifically to the women because, in a lot of cases, it's the women that are married to an unbelieving spouse. So oftentimes, if it's a man that is married to an unbelieving spouse, then over time, that woman generally will follow along with the spiritual leadership of the husband, but in many situations, it's reversed. Now, what I've seen over and over again is that when the husband is not a believer, the woman tends to stunt her spiritual role because she follows after or submits to his leadership.

## Your desire to get involved in church and the history of your small groups and hang out with all your Christian friends is now taking you further

Or his pace. Ladies or brothers, if you find yourself in the situation, whatever you do, continue to do all the things to foster your individual relationship with Christ even though your spouse is not interested at all in spiritual growth.

**Tip #7: Do not neglect short family responsibilities.**

What I mean here is this; oftentimes, whenever we are excited, we're on fire for Christ, and we want to go to church every night. We want to do all these things, we want to serve and attend ministries, and we're gone because we got this newfound commitment. We're like, "You know what? I'm going hard for Jesus Christ, and that's what I should be doing." Yet we're neglecting our family responsibilities. You do not want your husband to present church. You don't want him to resent you because you're always gone, and he's left doing all of the work, or she's left doing all of the work, or maybe they're left doing all the raising of the children, cooking the dinner, helping with the homework because now your desire to get involved in church and history of your small groups and hang out with all your Christian friends is taking you further and further away from your family responsibilities.

## Further away from your family responsibilities. Remember that you still have a major obligation as a husband and as a wife

Remember that you still have a major obligation as a husband and as a wife. When you stand before God, the judgment of God is going to hold you accountable for your role as a husband, a wife, a father, or a mother. So be careful not to neglect your family.

My friend, if you find yourself in this situation, hopefully, these seven tips, as well as the medical foundation for what God has to say, will help you navigate through this difficult situation. It is very difficult. I'm not going to make light of it, and that is the reason why if you're single watching this video, trust me, you do not want to be in this situation. The most important thing that you need to be looking for in a mate is a solid relationship with Jesus Christ. That's not the only thing, but my friend, that is the most important thing. So my brothers and sisters, hang strong, continue to pray, continue to serve, and continue to do all that you can. as a

## Further away from your family responsibilities, remember that you still have a major obligation as a husband or as a wife

Mary and non-believer. Now, to be totally fair, the Bible doesn't specifically say "don't date a non-believer" because dating isn't talked about in the Bible. However, marriage is specifically mentioned in the scripture, and it says, "do not marry a non-believer," in First Corinthians 7, verse 39. So, that's really clear, but what we want to do now is say, "Why? What's so dangerous about it? What's going on here?"

Well, the first thing we want to say is that all of God's commands are for our good. In Deuteronomy 10 to 13, that's exactly what God says. He says these commands are for your benefit. God knows what's right. God, He is perfect.

## Adam and Eve by saying. God's holding out on you. This command where he said, "Do not eat of this tree," is because he is holding out on you, and it is better for you to disobey God. Obey him

He's whole, He's unwounded, and He is perfect within Himself. Full of joy right now. He didn't need all the commands in the Bible for Himself; He made them for us. They are the guardrails of life, and they teach us what God wants for us. God wants good for us. God loves us, so these commands are not a punishment. They are not restrictions. In a way, these commands are for our good.

At the core of what caused Adam and Eve to sin in the beginning was the doubt that God's commands were actually for their good. When Satan tried to tempt them, he said, "You know, God knows that you'll become like Him if you eat this fruit." In other words, Satan tempted Adam and Eve by saying God's holding out on you. This command where he said, "Don't eat of this tree," that's actually because he's holding out on you, and it's actually better for you to disobey God, but that's a lie. Anytime we disobey the scriptures, we are hurting ourselves, and God doesn't want that for us. While it may feel very restrictive for God to say that a Christian should not be unequally yoked with a non-Christian, we first have to understand the foundational motive for who

## Because we were raised in this environment.

If you live in another part of the world, it's likely that your clothing will differ from those in America. This is because, culturally, we are shaped by the people around us. For instance, if you grow up in a certain area of town, your dialect might even be different from just a few miles away. We talk that way because we were raised in that environment. So, when you marry someone, you are committing to spending the rest of your life with that person. And when you're dating someone, it's extremely influential to be yoked with that person, so when

## Do not yoke yourself with somebody who is not trying to please God.

If you yoke yourself with somebody who isn't trying to please God, it's unrealistic to say that they won't affect you or turn you away from God. We are meant to shape one another, which is why He wants us to be. I'm saying Christians are supposed to be isolationists. We're not supposed to separate ourselves from the world and just stay away from everybody because they might affect us. However, we should have a mindset where we want to influence non-Christians, rather than be influenced by the world. We are not supposed to be of the world, but we will be living in it. So, it doesn't mean that as a Christian, you completely separate yourself from everyone who doesn't believe in Jesus; that would be extremely unloving and prideful, and that's not what God wants us to do. It's good to have relationships and connections with the world, but

## Now you cannot have a romantic relationship where you are not giving and taking.

In a romantic relationship, they need to be in such a way that they are not getting influenced by each other; instead, you are the one influencing them now. You cannot have a romantic relationship where you're not giving and taking; we are not being shaped and molded by one another; that's the point of marriage. And a good healthy friendship relationship is based on mutual give and take, and you don't want that with somebody who does not desire to please God. For example, Nehemiah 1326 talks about foreign women's influence on Solomon women, who did not want to please God. This is what it says was it not because of marriages like these that Solomon, king of Israel, sinned among the many nations? There was no king like him, his God loved him and made him king over all of Israel, but even he was led into sin by foreign women, so we can think that we have it all together and that we won't be influenced, but the reality is even Solomon was influenced by women who didn't love God. So don't try to fool yourself into thinking that you know

## Now you cannot have a romantic relationship where you are not giving and taking

When you link with someone, you can do something that's never been done in history. As Romans 8:8 says, those in the realm of the flesh cannot please God. Hebrews 11:6 also states that without faith, it is impossible to please God. Anyone who comes to him must believe that he exists and rewards those who earnestly seek him. In summary, if you link with a non-believer, the Bible clearly states that someone who doesn't believe in God and isn't trying to please him will not be able to please him. Linking with them will hurt your walk with the Lord. The next point is that the longer you two are together, the further your trajectory will go apart if you are truly following God and this person is not a Christian. Even if it seems like it'll work early on, and you have things in common and enjoy spending time with one another, and all of that might absolutely be true, you might genuinely have a good connection like that person that you really enjoy

## Do not live your life in a completely unique way.

They're respectful; they're not like over the top sinful or anything, and you're like what's the big deal this person seems fine well the reality is maybe right now your relationship's OK and it's not like causing you to overtly sin however the reality is we are all on a certain path in life. And right now, you guys might be very close to one another in your path oh as the years go on your path will become further and further apart. because you're heading away from, they're heading away from that and you're heading towards God so one of two things will happen you will. This can lead to either compromising on our beliefs or growing so far apart that the relationship becomes miserable. This is especially problematic in marriage when raising children, as differing views can cause conflict. One final point that is really important is Christians, and non-Christians view marriage differently.

## As a Christian with a biblical worldview, marriage has a very specific meaning. It is one of the highest representations of how Christ and the church love one another.

As a Christian with a biblical worldview, marriage is a symbolic representation of Christ's love for the church. Christ lays down his life for the church, and the church submits to and follows Christ. Marriage works best when we fit into those roles. Non-believer doesn't take that view because they don't believe in God, so they have a different understanding and belief of the meaning of marriage, which will dramatically affect how they interact with their spouse over the years, and the underlying motivations of their hearts. Always control and dictate the way that we live so. In summary, you will cause a lot of damage and it'll be very difficult. Jesus loves us and warns us not to marry non-Christians because the view of marriage is completely different. If you are a Christian and want to know how God will tell you who to marry.

## What we have produced help for marriage, it differentiate us from everyone else.

When I was a divorce mediator, I began helping couples with their marriages at the request of one couple. Instead of helping them get a divorce, I came up with a great template, and we sat and worked together for a few sessions. Although it didn't take long for them to see improvement, the husband returned to me several weeks later. He said, Paul, this stuff is great, but I can't do it. What am I going to do? I understand that breaking habits is very difficult. This topic is not about habits, but it's a layer above or beneath it depending on how you look at it, and that's what I discovered that differentiates the marriage foundation. What we have come up with for marriage helps differentiate us from everyone else, and that is that I realized if you don't master your mind, the chances of you being happy in your marriage or anywhere else in your life is a total crapshoot because you will depend upon external conditions to determine your happiness, which doesn't really make sense. If you think about it because we are souls

## A body and a mind is what we need.

We have a body and a mind, but we are souls. We know, or at least hope, that the attributes of the soul are ever-new joy and ever-increasing love; that's what being a soul is all about. However, our minds can get in the way. Now, your spouse is irritating you no matter what they do. You are thinking, 'Why?' You may even wonder if they can get it together or if they can stop irritating you. Here's the thing... Again, when you understand this, it will change your life. We have free will, so everything we perceive, hear, and see is filtered by our own determinations. Let's use this crazy example: An arsonist sees a fire and is excited, while a normal person hopes nobody gets hurt. The perception of what is going on outside is 100% up to you as an individual.

## What they are doing, or you could use this as a thread to go into your own mind.

Remember, it's not them that are causing your irritation. It's your filter that's allowing you to be irritated. Some people would suggest reframing their actions, changing the context, or using it as a thread to explore their own thoughts. Change how you perceive them entirely because what's really happening is that thought that you're having of being irritated is the problem it doesn't come before that's the thought, so if you change that thought So, what did. When I first learned about this, it was a humongous epiphany for me. I realized that, overall, marriage help cannot be achieved by simply talking about the couple's problems. This is because it's only how they perceive their problems, and their minds are getting in the way of what makes marriage work, which is love. It didn't get married because maybe you did for a green card because you wanted a better lifestyle and they had money. Maybe who knows, but it doesn't make any difference because we really all get married out of love is the reason for marriage love is the purpose of marriage. Happiness is important in marriage, but if we can't control our own thoughts, we can't blame our spouse. Remember, Jesus loves us so much.

## Prayer for any situation you're in now in your married life.

Father God, thank you for the opportunity to share your word with so many people who will read these words. Father God, thank you for the opportunity to share your Word with so many people who will read these words. We thank you for giving them the understanding to know what to do in this situation. Some of them, while reading this book, will see that their lives are better because they made the best decision. They followed your Word, went to church, and did what they had to do, and now they are happy. Many of them are happy because they know you and can testify to what you have done and will continue to do for them.

However, there are others who will make this decision but may not know how difficult it can be or that there may be difficulties in the relationship. I ask you, God, to give them your knowledge so they can choose according to your Word. When the time comes for them to act, may they be able to do so according to your Word. We thank you for your love and for the many people we pray for who will listen to your word and have their lives transformed.

We thank you for the opportunity to reach out to so many people, and I ask you, God, to bless them.

## For Adam, there was not found a helpmate who fit perfectly with him.

In marriage, some people don't understand what this means. But for Adam, there was not found a helpmate who fits perfectly with him. When the Lord sends someone to you, he has chosen that person for you. A spiritual union is essential, not just a physical one. Many people marry without this oneness in spirit, which can lead to problems.

Verse 22 of the Bible passage is powerful. It says, "And the rib which the Lord God had taken from man made a woman." The Lord did not breathe a second time, indicating that the woman was already a part of the man.

Marriage is the bedrock of society and an essential component of social harmony. As a therapist, I have talked to many people about their marriages. In my own 33-year marriage, I have experienced the joys of caring for someone and being cared for in return.

## Not everyone is going to see a vision of his wife.

Not everyone will see a vision of his wife. Seeing no vision does not mean you are not spiritual. Sorry, man, now look up. Not everybody is going to see a vision. You were standing there when you suddenly saw a woman in need, and God said, 'Arise, why are you sitting here? Go and take your position.' He said, 'No, Lord, but I am weak.' I have to say, no, you are not weak. You have the strength to fulfill God's purpose for your life. If that is what you are waiting for, you may be disappointed.

## You must contribute to the kingdom of God.

Please listen. Because God cannot plant a genuine passion without your participation. What kind of house are you? Are you a faithful worker? I'm not talking about Charles, but you're not contributing anything to the Kingdom of God. You seem to want to leave every harvest to others who are working hard for it. To truly contribute, you must genuinely participate in the Kingdom. On Monday, you may suddenly find out channeling desire. Please remove the loss from it if you see that. I notice that you have an unusual desire and passion for helping patients. Come patience unusual desire, now watch this. When this happens, brothers are too early. Many of you don't have self-control because once you feel anything, you land it till the lady lumps it back at you. Be temperate. Don't just say, "Let me ask first," before another person comes and asks you. You don't know whether she's in a relationship. You don't know whether and what; you just go and disgrace yourself. The Lord told me you are the one to say sorry. We're getting married next week.

## Take your responsibilities.

You carry your responsibilities. Now, you may feel stupid or irresponsible, but it won't last forever. There are different seasons in life, my brothers and sisters. So, God can use a simple, godly desire. I've seen this in many ladies. When you connect with someone's spirit and build a friendship over time, it leads to many productive things. Some people don't even understand the concept of friendship. They just come and see a stranger and say, "You are my wife. I will marry you. Go and pray about it. I will be here tomorrow." What sort of nonsense is that? It's very rude. You may not know it, but it has worked for others. But I'm telling you, it's very rude. You don't walk up to a lady and just say, "You are my wife. Pray about it." That's bullying.

This is a Christian household. Especially if you're a man of God or a great person, don't use your position to intimidate ladies. This book is about marriage. What I do like about it is that we explain all the facts about marriage, such as the visions about marriage, how to handle problems in marriage, and how to do so many things so that you can have a successful marriage and resolve some problems.

## It is going to be good for everyone to have knowledge about this book.

You can look for people who have a plan for the future. I can say that we give all the guidelines about marriage, and I know this book is going to be loved by everybody, even those who have been married for 50 years or those who have been used to the 60s. Whatever it is, I believe it's going to be good for everyone to have knowledge about this book. You're going to love it, and the other thing is, it's going to be affordable. If someone learns something tonight, they might say, "I'm passionate." There are many of us who find ourselves having a godly, genuine desire for someone, and some of us are very embarrassed. Suddenly, you are embarrassed that somebody you always play with is a guy. "Why am I like this?"

Now you go to pray "kababi shatara."

## The prophetic clear means either prophecy or the ministry of the Holy Spirit in your life.

It was that someone was listening to me. I already know because I want to talk about roads and codes of conduct, so I'll pass on number 2. The prophetic God has also positioned the prophetic to help the man in locating the woman. The prophetic clear means either prophecy or the ministry of the Holy Spirit in your life, and please, I must balance this because that's what brought the issue of fission. I saw fission, I saw it, I saw this. Hallelujah, hold on. Let me use the opportunity for balance. On the right now, look up, everybody.

## It must be handled with maturity because marriage is a great issue. Are you getting my

God does not appoint you as a spiritual matchmaker, moving around and looking at people and saying, 'Eureka! If you're considering someone for marriage, whether you're sitting behind them in church or have a dream about them, it must be handled with utmost maturity because marriage is a significant issue. Are you getting my point? Now, you can warn an innocent lady and tell her,

'You know, that's I saw Mama looking at you,' and all of a sudden, it becomes an artificial desire, especially if it falls at a point in her life where she's from, or if there is, you know what I'm talking about, right? And then at that point, all of a sudden, this lady now begins to cry herself, and maybe left her through Mama

## People engage in all kinds of skills and spiritual activities in their bid to recover back the Kingdom.

Almost authority and look and say, 'I have seen it.' If it does not happen, quote the UN. Then, she sees the guy's computational cut like, 'Wasn't it deposit?' And the ladies now want, 'Oh God, what is going on? This is my husband here. Leaving me alone.' And people engage in all kinds of skills and spiritual activity in their bid to recover back the Kingdom. Does not leave us in confusion. Don't you, on the other hand, neglect the place of the prophetic. There are so many people I have seen in my dreams and ambitions, waiting before. In fact, when I saw it, they did not even know themselves. Even me when I saw

## Marriage and prophecy.

I was surprised when the hand of God connected them. You know why I'm saying this? When it comes to marriage, even prophecy can change. So when you die, people may now say,

'Kasham, stand up. It's a tall guy. One day, he will sit down two seats close to you. Write it down. His name is Adrian. If you miss him, you have missed your husband.' Five years later, Kasham is still going around hoping, 'Andrew, where are you?' Adriel is planning his wedding. Are you getting my point? They don't know that Adrian is the one who will come. They told me, 'Atrial fair, it's any guy that comes.' I don't want Kashamu to sit forever without a husband because somebody gave her the wrong prophecy. Are you getting what I'm saying now? There are many of us who may be sitting down right now with the wrong prophecies. Please be careful. Prophecies must be designed and balanced cheerfully. Listen to me, listen.

## It was God himself that appointed Saul to be king. He can do the same for your marriage.

It was God himself that appointed Saul to be king. Is that true? It was the same God that rejected Saul as king. True or false? It was God that appointed Moses to take God's people to the land flowing with milk and honey. Did God tell him he would not get there? Later on, it was the same God that stopped him. So be careful. That you saw a lady named shown is no guarantee that you must marry her. There are many factors that might make must come together: alignment. Are you getting my point? There is alignment. There is parental approval and all of these other factors. For others, maybe tribal differences or whatever it is. There are factors together, so

## In a guided atmosphere of the world and spiritual maturity, prophecy can be enormously powerful. Hallelujah!

It doesn't just work automatically. Please get this revelation. If you don't get it, you are going to fool yourself into error. However,in a guided atmosphere of the world and spiritual maturity, prophecy can be very powerful. Hallelujah!

Prophecy can be powerful in helping you understand your spouse. Number three, please play my divine connection just like that. No fusion, no nothing. Divine connection. For instance, we now give both Emmy and Timmy trust. Give them a song to score together. His twin, his workers empty, but the Spirit of God. Come on now! The Spirit of God, Toy Washington Riaza, and not much making. I'm just giving an example. Hallelujah! And in the course of the Riaza, they have a chance to discuss life and find...

## Do not be a dead person in the house of God.

Out that there is a connection in ideologies all of a sudden family supernaturally starts having credit that's good cooperating with the events to happen somebody just sent 15 whereas they wouldn't have sent 1/5 every time you pray towards that relationship Taiwan are you getting the point now ? Let me tell you something. In the House of God, your spouse is not lost. The Bible says, "He that lives by the altar sheets by the altar." So, when you wait for two hours, or she's delayed to go, the only seat left is where the family is seated. Everyone says divine connection always happens. It absolutely does. They've been inviting you for years, but suddenly in 2014, God brings you. They said, 'Turn around and hope for one another, and good things happen. Your wife is Anusha. You're both happy.'

## The Bible said he broke bread, and their eyes were open.

The Bible says, 'He broke bread, and their eyes were open the sister, you've been seeing everything. They're not just the son of man; the season has come. Theron was moving around and he went to play a band while this is double back God will say just save Ruth you will soon go to Naomi's vineyard ASAP do you know many of you because of your marriage God you from you got 200 and something they didn't give you admission there God we located you and brought you in this season everybody said divine connection that's how we meet destiny help us that's how many of you gave your life to Christ you were strolling around, and you heard a preacher preaching you just said let me enter and listen to the message define connection and you met destiny that's how some of you came to colonial it's one of the principles, in fact, let me tell you the truth is one of the strongest ways that corporates are connected together something in the House of God touch your breasts, and Lord connect me to find

## Your spouse needs to be pleased with your marriage.

It's likely that your spouse is unhappy with your marriage as it stands right now. So, in other words, your spouse isn't necessarily unhappy with you, but he or she certainly isn't pleased with your marriage. That means that a positive change, even if it happens on its own, is likely to change your spouse's feelings about the marriage and make them more likely to buy back in and recommit to a future together.

Fact number 2 is that you and your partner communicate in a revolving stimulus, essentially what's called a response pattern.

## I know this might sound very sciency but let me explain briefly

I know this might sound very sciency but let me explain briefly what this means because it's actually not that complicated. A response pattern is basically just a cycle where what you do and say is the stimulus, and

then your spouse's reaction is the response, and then you react to their reaction, and so on. The cycle continues, and of course, the same thing occurs when your partner does or says something; you react, they react to your reaction, and so on. Over time, the two of you have developed a pattern of these common actions and reactions, but when the stimulus changes, the response will also change, and this is great news. What it usually means is that changing your behavior will impact your partner's reaction and the entire relationship.

## Do not get into arguments

Now, let me explain these two facts a little bit further by using a simple example. Let's imagine that you and your partner always get into arguments about spending holidays with him. You supposedly want to drive five hours every Christmas to have dinner with his or her family, but you hate these big family dinners. Each time your spouse asks you to go on these holiday family trips, you refuse to go, and complain about having to attend, and your spouse then becomes upset. Of course, a big argument ensues, and your spouse threatens to take the kids and go without you.

## Unhappiness can make the marriage suffer

And then the argument spirals into a bigger debate over your general unwillingness to ever do what your partner wants. Now, in this example, the original issue or the stimulus is your spouse's desire to visit family at Christmas, and the reaction, of course, is your refusal to do so. They are supposed to then react to your reaction with a further complaint, an argument follows, and the pattern continues. In the end, you both wind up unhappy, and your marriage suffers because of this whole fiasco.

## What to avoid in other for your marriage to stay healthy and happy

Now, when this happens regularly, both of you are going to be unhappy with the marriage and your life in general. I realize, at this point, you might be wondering, OK, how is all of this actually good news for my marriage? Well, simply put, in the response pattern that

I just described, you have the power to disrupt the negative cycle by making a change to the initial action or to the reaction. This, by itself, can actually help you improve the health of your marriage without any involvement from your spouse.

Let's go back to the example that I just described a minute ago. Now, what if you had simply agreed to visit your in-laws on Christmas, just like your spouse wanted? Well, then, the reaction from your partner would now be a positive one rather than a negative one. The ensuing argument would no longer happen at all, and therefore there wouldn't be any negative interaction with your spouse in the first place. This, of course, is going to be a far better outcome for your marriage than if you had put up a fight over the issue.

## Your spouse's demand is particularly important

This all happens without your spouse being aware of you really doing anything differently at all. Obviously, there are times when you can't or even shouldn't simply give in to your spouse's demands and do what he or she wants, but in this particular example, perhaps you can maybe agree to go and visit your in-laws this year but not the following year or maybe you can agree to stay home for Christmas but visit your spouse's family over the Easter weekend instead. Now I know this sounds pretty obvious and insignificant on the surface, but this type of content conflict resolution can actually be invaluable.

## Because it can help you save your marriage

It can help you save your marriage alone without your spouse's help. Simply put, by making a small change to your own behavior, your partner will need to use their coping mechanism, and the negative cycle of reactions and actions no longer needs to occur at all. If this happens often enough, a new pattern of behaviors emerges, and assuming that new actions and reactions are positive, then your overall relationship is going to be healthier as a result. Now at the beginning of this video, I promised to tell you why, sometimes, it can even be better to work on saving your marriage without your spouse being aware or involved at all in the process. It is true. There are actually a couple of reasons why this is often the case. The first reason is that communication isn't always beneficial. See, in many cases, talking with your partner about the problems in your marriage can actually make matters worse rather than better.

## Talking through issues tends to simply reinforce your spouse's belief that the marriage does indeed have real problems

I know this might seem counterintuitive, but talking through issues tends to simply reinforce your spouse's belief that marriage does indeed have real problems. It helps your supposed to focus on those specific problems. In other words, it's usually better for you and your spouse to be spending quality positive time together than it is to revisit the same issues and arguments over and over again by discussing them together. By taking the first steps on your own, you can help to create this more positive atmosphere in your marriage without reminding your spouse about the problems that led you to this point. Now, the second benefit is that when you are working on your marriage by yourself, you can begin to make changes in media, unlike traditional marriage counseling.

## It might take weeks or even months to make progress, especially if you are only seeing therapists

It might take weeks or even months to make progress, especially if you are only seeing therapists. You know, every so often, change to your own behavior and to the stimulus-response cycle that I described earlier. They can begin immediately, and that means that you could begin to work on making your marriage today.

So there you have it, folks! Not only is it possible to start fixing your marriage alone and without your spouse's help, but it's also actually sometimes even beneficial to do so. Now I do want to warn you that what I've discussed in this video is how I'm going to teach you how to prevent such a long time.

## It now with rebuilding a broken marriage is a rocky broke sometimes; things can get worse before they get better

With the proper guidance, help, and attitude, it is possible to turn your marriage around despite how thousands of so-called hopeless companies turn it around, and I know exactly how they did it. With that being said, rebuilding a broken marriage is a rocky broke; sometimes, things can get worse before they get better. It takes a lot of devotion on your part to make things better. However, I promise to tell you what not to do now. The vast majority of married couples that

I coach commit almost all of these very damaging mistakes I'm about to talk about. I know that some of you may be in a situation where your spouse isn't willing to work on the marriage, but I'm going to tell you why that's actually and why it's even more important for you to learn these common mistakes before you go down the road of building a newer happier. Some of the stuff you may already know, but it's important to remember these mistakes before you cause any further damage to your marriage, and these are tips that will have an immediate impact on your relationship. I like to call these mistakes "big marital mistakes."

## Do not feel desperate

Big marital mistake number one: Initiating needless conflict with your spouse

When you're trying to fix a broken marriage, and you're feeling desperate, chances are that things spiral out of control very easily. I think you know what I'm talking about. You think that if you could just talk to your spouse about all your problems and find common ground, your marriage will magically fix itself and get better, but usually, this isn't the case, and it's not how it happens. Now while communicating with your spouse is important in rebuilding a marriage, what your marriage does not need right now is another argument or fight. Even if your partner says something antagonizing or wants to bring up a touchy, sticky issue at the moment, just do your best to avoid conflict politely. Don't ignore your spouse or discount any other concerns, but you do need to ensure that the discussion doesn't end up in a screening match.

## Be polite, and you will resolve this issue

You can just say something along the lines of, "You know, I know this is a real concern right now, and I want to resolve this issue. Can we discuss this later?" Be polite to defer the argument. In general, it's best to try and be as nonconfrontational as possible, at least for now, until you learn how to manage and handle your arguments later.

It's what I call my "dispute diffusing system" a little bit later in this video, but if you do have any questions or concerns about this comma, especially in public. I know that when emotions are running rampant, people tend to say or do things they'll inevitably regret. I'm sure you know exactly what I'm talking about. Certain times, your spouse may say or do things that will make you feel angry, upset, or sad.

## Get control of your emotions

You need to do your absolute best to control your own emotions at these times. Showing negative emotions is only going to make matters worse, and unfortunately, doing so will help you sign those divorce papers even sooner, so for now, it's extremely important to just try and remain calm and live to fight another Big marital mistake #3: Making drastic changes to your life or your habits.

When your marriage is in a rut, it can affect your entire life, your work, or your school immensely. You suddenly take the back seat, and in some cases, so does your health and nutrition. For the time being, you must retain a sense of normalcy whenever possible if you begin floundering in life.

## Do not be depressed

I can guarantee you that your marriage will begin flowering even more. After all, nobody wants a spouse who's always depressed, angrier, and rose. Show how confident, strong, and bold you are by showing the world that nothing can faze you. By doing so, you'll not only appear much more attractive to your spouse, but you'll also ensure that you don't damage yourself anymore.

Big marital mistake #4: The navigator spouse

Now, this is similar to mistake number one, and you'll want to avoid any sort of confrontation whenever possible. It's normal to be annoyed at your spouse every once in a while when your marriage is in trouble. Small conversations can easily lead to larger ones, and the last thing you need at this point is another pointless argument. So the next time your spouse does something that annoys you, hold it in. This is the time when you start fixing your marriage on your own.

## Outline the mistakes

This isn't an exhaustive list of marital mistakes. Now that we have an outline, I'm going to wait for all the married couples that need to fix their marriage or those that are thinking about marrying one day because some people plan to get married, but they are already thinking about the situation. Maybe they have someone they know, or maybe they have some good and bad experiences at the same time. They say they are going through it, but one thing that cannot help them do it is the Bible Addison. "Why we're going to pray that the Holy Ghost cannot bless every readers of this book because we already give you all the details that you're going to need to do. Whether you are not married or are already married, whoever is going to access this book, will have the guidance

## Holy Spirit comes into our marriage

They need to have a good marriage. We're going to pray the Holy Ghost God, "If you're able to guide us and everything that we do because if we leave our thanks to God like a married family, believe me, God is going to make it work. There's nothing that is impossible for God to do because, in everything, we have to consider God, the God of heaven and earth, the God that created heaven and earth. God says one thing, and I want to repeat it. He said that the world and everything that is in it is for Him. That means God has all the wishes of the power that they would ever have.

## Do not poison the marriage. It is created by God in the Garden of Eden

We come to the conclusion of this book. We used so many ideas and so many examples to help understand our viewpoint because we did this long ago, and a theology school that was our TCS that was the main idea we chose.

Marriage is instituted by God. God is the one that created marriage. The Garden of Eden, this is where he did it for Adam and Eve. Today we tell you about what other people say about noise, like apostle Paul, and then we remember Jesus went to marriage when there was no wine, and Jesus did a miracle there when he made the best one.

## They are going to find out what to do to save their marriage

We have some people that God blessed, and we know if we want to say their name, we're going to choose to give you a lot of passages that talk about marriage, , I'm going to say, is a documentary that we're going to need to have in order to be good. Some people don't need to know everything in the world, but when they need to read this book, they're going to find what to do in order to save their marriage writing this book about my own marriage.

I'm not writing this book about someone I know in the marriage. Writing this book is about my spiritual knowledge of God and the Bible. This is how I'm writing this book, not for my personal example.. I want to make sure bring something that maybe they going togoing to if they love this book. They're going to fight to save their marriage because marriage has never been something that was easy from ancient times to the present moment. It has never been easy from now to the present moment. It's never been easy because, believe me, marriage is something very nice. I want to say one thing about finances. Like to be wise. It's good to have money. This is my own word, the author's word. To be wise, you need to have some money. What I mean by that Solomon, in the bible, is the man that we see as the wisest man in the world.

# You, your Marriage, and your family in God's side

But according to his judgments and if he had a lot of money, he was a rich man. That means he was a very wise man because sometimes, to make a decision, it's not going togoing to be with the word. It has to accompany by money because those that know the word of God know what I'm talking about. Sometimes in church, we used to help people, but how do we help people? Sometimes someone in need even gives some advice to that person.

# They are going to fight to save their marriage because marriage has never been something that was easy from the ancient time to the present moment

We need to help them financially to make them practice what we are teaching because sometimes you can say something, but that does not mean that is going to be happening because there are certainly other problems. If you cannot solve this problem, then the main problem will always be there, so that means withholding some big problems; there are some little ones. You should be able to solve finances. Marriage is the biggest thing. I am not going to say the biggest problem, but it is the most important thing. Everyone who is going to be married needs to have money. When I say not only money going to save your marriage

## A marriage that has money is a marriage where they are going to know some exceptionally good days, some joyful days

But a marriage that has money is a marriage where they are going to know some exceptionally good days, some joyful days. They are going to make some great memories, believe me. I do not want to talk about saving your marriage. You need money because some people have a very wonderful marriage, and then they do not have money; they have love. They accept the situation however it is, and they have an exceptionally good life, but we want to make sure we emphasize because that is going to be the plan; that is what we are going to do to be prepared. It will be prepared to have all the things that are needed for that because if we take some examples about other people who make that preparation and then they have prepared before they get in, believe me, when

## We are living in a time where sometimes, even though you do everything by yourself on your own, that does not mean you are going to have the outcome that you wanted

Finance is not coming as an issue. They might have other issues but not financial issues, so we're going to say. We know that the time we are living in now, it's not easy for people to get what they need because some people want to go to school, they graduated, they have degrees, they have licenses but they don't have a job. We are living in a time where sometimes, even though you do everything by yourself, on your own, that doesn't mean you're going to have the outcome that you wanted.

## Prayer for Individuals in marriage

That isn't why we want to make sure we do what we have to do because God can make them happy. This is what I want to say today, so let's go away because we're not going to only write this book about what we know and what the bible says, but we want to invite the Holy Spirit for whoever cannot participate in this book so that you're going to be able to, and pray with us. That is going to be like. We see that the bible is inspired, but we want to make sure we add the Holy Spirit to our world because we are Christians. We need to live a Christian life defined in the bible. We are spirit, and we have to live according to the spirit, Father.

God, You are holy, we worship You this morning, and I thank You for everything that You do for us. We have the opportunity to meet people in the world, wherever they are, and be able to read this book because we have come to a conclusion. We want to show we pray because prayer opens doors that are closed, and then through prayers, there can be miracles. That is the reason why; in this moment, I want to pray for everyone that will have this book and may be living in this situation and need some change, or some other people may be planning to get married. May God bless them.

## Bibliography

The new international study Bible Theological Dictionary of the New Testament volume second edited by G Kittel theological revised King James GD Douglas

The New International Dictionary of the bible's grand rapid Michigan Zondervan publishing 1987 Edward W Goodrich and John R. call and burger to eat the NIV exhaustive concordance grand rapid Michigan 49530 Zondervan publishing in 1990.

Praise the Lord, now I'm going to start with the wedding. Ephesians five verses 20-22,

*"Wives submit to your husband as to the Lord for the husband is the head of the wife as Christ is the head of the church, his body of which you receive, you know what I did in the church so submit to Christ so also wives should submit to their husbands and everything."*

## Do not live according to the flesh

In the church today, I see so many Christians that are struggling to live like Christ. They want to, but they're in such slavery to their sins. It reminds me so much of what Paul talks about in Romans Chapter 7, verse 18, where he says, "For I know that nothing good dwells in me, that is in my flesh, for I have the desire to do what is right, but not the ability to carry it out for I do not do the good. I want but the evil I do not want is what I keep on doing,"

You see, so many Christians are living this life, and it leads to frustration, leads to discouragement, a sense of failure, a sense of guilt, and then these Christians end up defining themselves and their Christian walk by these things, so the reason why it's very obvious is that people are living out of the flesh

## Renew your mind, do not live by the flesh

People living out of a place of works, and they've reduced this living word of God to a book of dead principles that they try to apply but don't have the power to do. It's exactly the same as trying to stick pieces of fruit on a tree rather than allowing a tree to just produce fruit naturally, and then people reduce this Christian life to this "Oh, well, no one is perfect" sort of mindset which allows them to remain without. It gives them permission to stay where they are.

They define their walk by their experiences and by the way people living are around them rather than God's word, and they have such a sin consciousness that it actually becomes their identity. They're struggling in their flesh, and they're putting on their Christian base, and they're trying to do good, and they're just failing over and over. If you're struggling with this, the good news is that you're struggling with this because there are people out there who don't even care about trying to live like Christ. You obviously care enough if you're struggling with this, and God can use that. That's a place to start from; the desire to want to live like that. You see. the answer to living this life is actually very simple. It's living in the spirit and living from a place of grace, not from a place of works. It's a transformation rather than just trying to improve upon the old self. The bible says in Two Corinthians 5:17

## If anyone is in Christ, he is a new creation

If anyone is in Christ, he is a new creation. Behold, the old has passed away, the new has come, and this is a complete transformation about being. It's a change that is about solving our livesHere, it is not so different than what you're thinking. It's a revelation of your identity. That is a place where you can live abundantly, or it comes as natural as breathing, and when you've done your work, it becomes straightening and strong. The spirit is working through you to produce the life that you want to live. This is really great, but how do I actually employ these in my life that I've transformed, and I'm living this out every day?

The answer is simply to avoid this work as an accident, and the first step is to backup home safely. I do not have the power to do so. That's the first place. That's a fantastic place to be because that's a place of humility. That's a place of dependence on God. When you're in that place, He can come in and work through you, and you don't want to run to the gospel when trouble comes and try and reply to these principles in your own strength to overcome it. You want to be with you every day, and you want the gospel to be alive inside of you, living and active when the crisis comes with the situation.

## Roman 12:2

Your mind and your heart, we need to love God with all our hearts.

"And do not live according to the present world. Do not be conformed to this world, to the system of this world. Respect the authority. But do not dress like them, act like them, but be transformed by renewing of the mind."

New Mind, this is the prescription for all the problems you might have. Add this verse to your marriage, and you will see how God will change things for you. Isaia 40

Made in the USA
Columbia, SC
19 April 2025

56822770R00117